PRACTICAL WISDOM

FROM

KABBALAH

AND

EDGAR CAYCE

ELLIOT CHIPRUT

GOLDEN KINGDOM PRESS
DELAND, FLORIDA

DEDICATION

To my wife Rae Karen,
with all my heart.

ACKNOWLEDGMENTS

A heartfelt thanks to our Creator God and the Holy Spirit for all of the precious Light we share.

Very special thanks to my extraordinary wife, Rae Karen, for all your love, inspiration, patience, and expertise. We are truly one.

My deepest appreciation to Charles Thomas Cayce for passing along the idea for this book. You are indeed a blessing.

Many, many thanks to all my unseen heavenly angels and my earth angels, Mary Luckie, Gerda von der Oelsnitz, Joni Taccetta, Jim DeVauld, Deb and Rex Hauck, David Hauck, Drew and Jerry Ivey, Steve Camhi, Debra Schultz, Pat and Bill Davis for all your loving support. May your Light shine forever.

My sincerest gratitude to my stepson, David Livesay, for all your help. Your vision and courage will be long remembered.

And a lasting thank you to my parents, Victoria and Isaac, for all your love and for giving me a foundation of Light. Forever will you remain in my heart.

TABLE OF CONTENTS

INTRODUCTION

There is so much talk today about different dimensions, parallel universes and higher vibrations. The most important thing to know, without getting too technical, is that *all is one*.

Yes, there is a spiritual plane of existence as well as our physical plane. This spiritual plane Kabbalah calls The Endless World, Upper World, or the world where all things occur before they occur here in the physical world. It also says this Upper World does not act until the lower world, the world of man, acts.

On a percentage ratio, *the physical world is only one percent of our True Reality, while the spiritual, or Endless World, is 99 percent.*

When I first heard this, it put a completely different perspective on things here in the physical world. To me it made sense. I had an inner knowing that it was true.

The study of Kabbalah can be quite vast and intense, as it actually is the wisdom of the mechanics of all creation, the blueprint of the universe. It is the oldest wisdom in the world. Although it stems from the ancient Jewish tradition, it is universal in its application.

The word itself in Hebrew means "to receive," in order to share. It is a most important work needing to be done on self.

Kabbalah is for all souls seeking the truth and freedom that comes from within. The freedom from our ego or lower self.

Along with the wisdom from the Edgar Cayce Readings, which parallel the truths of Kabbalah, and a little wisdom from some other complementary sources, this book is a "practical tools" approach to the basic challenges and desires in life. It will help attune us to the essence and importance of behavioral Kabbalah and The Tree of Life. It will reveal some of the secrets within ourselves that have been hidden from mankind for so many years.

The terminology used is simple to understand and easy to apply to everyday living. Its application will bring miraculous results to any person interested in changing their life for the better, by adding more Light to their being as well as removing darkness from the earth. It has helped me immensely to grow spiritually.

The Kabbalah information given provides methods for connecting to spiritual Light from the Upper World. Most of it is a derivative of the Zohar (The Book of Splendor), written by Rabbi Shimon bar Yochai 2,000 years ago. The Zohar, one of the two principle sources of the Kabbalists, is the mystical translation of the Torah, the first five books of Moses in the Old Testament.

The Zohar explains that the Light of the Creator is endless and never changes.

When our lower world disconnects from the Upper World (the Light of the Creator) through negative thoughts and behavior, we experience darkness in our lives.

This occurs each time we give in to the will of our ego instead of using *resistance,* a key concept in personal transformation. We make and hold the connection to the Upper World when we master our ego drives and perform positive actions prompted by our soul.

Some of the great Kabbalists in history to use these teachings include Patriarchs Abraham, Isaac and Jacob. It was Abraham who first received it 4,000 years ago as the Book of Formation, the Sefer Yetzirah, the other principle resource of the Kabbalists, helping him to understand the oneness of God. Moses used it as well. Jesus taught it to his disciples who tried to help bring Kabbalah's teachings to the people. Plato, Mohammed and Pythagoras also used it, as did Sir Isaac Newton, Shakespeare, Jung and many other great thinkers of the world.

Who Was Edgar Cayce?

Edgar Cayce, known as the "Sleeping Prophet," was a remarkable American seer and spiritual healer. He was born in 1877 on a farm near Hopkinsville, Kentucky.

For forty-three years of his adult life, Cayce demonstrated the uncanny ability to put himself into some kind of self-induced sleep state by lying down on a couch, closing his eyes, and folding his hands over his stomach. He was then able to place his mind in contact with all time and space, the universal source.

From this state he could vocally respond to questions asked of him from "What are the secrets of the universe?" to "How can I remove a wart?"

The responses, which were written down by his secretary, Gladys Turner, who did most of the steno transcribing, came to be called "readings." His wife, Gertrude, would ask the questions on behalf of the recipient of the reading.

Many readings were also given to people long distance whom he had never met. Each person who received a reading was assigned a number, in place of their name, in order to insure privacy. Each reading has that number attached to it. He charged very little for his readings because of his sincere desire to help those in need.

Cayce's accuracy was truly amazing. As a medical diagnostician, he helped thousands of people with diseases ranging from boils to insanity, saving or changing lives when all seemed hopeless. He is the most well documented psychic, with over 14,000 readings covering 10,000 subjects. The majority of these topics deal with five categories: Health-Related Information; Philosophy and Reincarnation; Dreams and Dream Interpretation; ESP and Psychic Phenomena; Spiritual Growth, Meditation and Prayer.

In his best-selling biography, *There Is A River* by Thomas Sugrue, Cayce spoke of the old mystery religions: "The Jewish faith had a secret doctrine. It was called 'cabala.' The students who learned it were called 'initiates,' and these were the high priests. They learned the esoteric part of the religion, and the people were given the exoteric version: they were given the same fundamental philosophy and the same moral code, but with a simple explanation."

What you are about to read is the simple explanation of spiritual wisdom.

PART ONE

IT'S ALL ABOUT LIGHT

Chapter 1

THE POWER OF LIGHT

In these uncertain times of high un-employment, financial unrest, global chaos and elusive security, we all can use some help in achieving inner peace.

The study and application of Kabbalah has dramatically changed my life. It began when my wife Karen and I received a book on Kabbalah from our dear friend, Gerda. The title was *A Wish Can Change Your Life*. At that time our lives were filled with challenges on many levels, mostly financial. Our inner guidance was to trust in God and not try to make things happen, or force the river.

Karen began to apply the weekly techniques working with the Kabbalah concepts. The changes that came were so profound, we were both guided to pursue Kabbalah further.

The Association for Research and Enlightenment (A.R.E.), the organization started by Edgar Cayce over seventy-five years ago, located in Virginia Beach, had behavioral Kabbalah classes on video tape available in their library. We checked them out and opened the door to learning more. It has been our experience over the years that when our souls needed to find something for our inner growth, the spiritual energy in the A.R.E. library amazingly led us to it.

After much study with the tapes, we then started a weekly study group at our home. This ultimately led to applying for a scholarship from the publisher of the Zohar to acquire the 23 volumes, which we were unable to afford at that time. A month later, to our surprise, the Zohar arrived in a large brown carton on our doorstep. The Light had come!

Soon we were both awakened separately at different times in the middle of the night to read and scan the Zohar, which was in Aramaic with Hebrew letters and the English translation.

The Hebrew letters are packets of Light energy. Scanning them brings in the Light. You don't even have to understand Hebrew to receive the benefits.

We started feeling a shift in our energy fields. A peaceful lightness came over us. The Zohar is very powerful unto itself.   Just having the books in your home can bring more Light, blessings and protection.

What I am about to share with you now is not meant to be a self-glorification, but rather a glorification of the power of the Light from our Heavenly Creator.

While doing the Kabbalah work, we had our first money miracle in January 2006 when a relative gifted us with an unexpected check for $10,000. This was a tremendous help at that hour as we were living on a shoestring.

Daily, we continued scanning and reading the Zohar, and practicing the Kabbalah principles we had learned.

In March 2006, we had another miracle when I received a phone call from Charles Thomas Cayce, then the CEO of the A.R.E., to write this book on Kabbalah and Cayce. He had heard me speak about Kabbalah at the weekly Edgar Cayce Work Group meetings I had been attending. I am a student of the Edgar Cayce Readings for over thirty years, which has had a profound effect on my spiritual transformation.

Another incredible money miracle occurred in December of 2006. We were still being financially challenged. My personal debt to the songwriter's credit union was quite substantial, leaving both Karen and myself, basically, with very little income to live on. To our pleasant surprise, without even asking, I received a large songwriter's advance against royalties to pay off the loan at the credit union. That advance has now been paid off as well. The Light had come again.

My personal experience with following this practical everyday version of Kabbalah's principles, and the Edgar Cayce readings, has given me more peace, love, joy, prosperity and understanding than ever before.

As we become agents of the Light of the Creator, we can help to shift the critical mass consciousness necessary for world transformation into peace and oneness.

Chapter 2

THE REAL WORLD

Let us briefly go back to the beginning of creation to help us understand more of the Real World concept.

According to Kabbalah, there is One Force. They call this the Light of the Creator, or God. As Rabbi Isaac Luria, the 16th Century Kabbalist, wrote:

"Know that before the emanations were emanated and the created were created, the exalted and simple Light filled the entire existence, and there was no empty space whatsoever."

The Cayce readings support this:

"Spirit is the First Cause, the primary beginning, the motivative influence—as God is Spirit." (262-123) "All power, all force, is a manifestation of that which is termed the God-consciousness." (601-11) "...God moved and said, 'Let there be Light,' and there was Light. Not the

7

Light of the sun, but rather that of which, through which, in which every soul had, has, and ever has its being." (5246-1)

Cayce explained, "What is Light? That which, through which, in which may be found all things, out of which all things come. Thus the first of everything which may be visible in earth, in heaven and in space is of that Light, is that Light." (2533-8)

Kabbalah says Light, which is actually the energy that comes from God, is His positive attributes such as Joy, Love, Peace, Harmony, Total Fulfillment, Oneness, and Sharing.

The Light, lacking nothing, had a desire for companionship to fulfill its giving nature. It separated itself into an immense number of sparks of Light, creating a receiver, or 'Vessel' (us) in Kabbalistic terms, with which to share all of its attributes of fulfillment.

Each of these sparks of Light was given free will. The Vessel was not a physical entity at this time but rather an intelligent, non-material essence. Its nature was an infinite Desire to Receive. This sharing of Light by the Creator, and the receiving of Light by the Vessel, was the name of this glorious game for a very long time.

The Vessel was becoming more and more like the Light.

Kabbalah calls this incredible unity of sharing and receiving, The Endless World, or total perfection. The infinite giving and receiving of fulfillment.

Then an amazing thing happened along the way that changed everything.

The Vessel, in the process of becoming more and more like the Light, now acquired the God-like desire *to want to share fulfillment as well as receive it.* To be the *cause* of its own happiness.

But this presented a major problem.

There was no place to express this newly acquired desire, as the Creator wants only to share and not receive, for He has and is everything.

This was the beginning of the seed of negative expressions that accompany unearned good fortune. The only way in which the Vessel could remove these negative expressions, and fulfill this sharing desire, was to stop receiving the Light, to push it back and resist it.

This is what science calls the "Big Bang," and what Kabbalah calls "Resistance."

The moment this occurred, which both say happened approximately 15 billion years ago, the Light lovingly withdrew and created an empty space that allowed for this experience.

A Point of Darkness

The Endless World now contained a point of darkness, time and space, for the Vessel's next unfoldment.

This darkness, or almost darkness, was created with ten curtains, each one blocking the glorious Light, which is everywhere always.

These are the Ten Sefirot (Hebrew word for Spheres), or the Tree of Life, divine emanations, the aspects of God. This is where 99 percent of our reality resides. The hidden dimensions which is the true source of all joy, wisdom and enlightenment. These are the same ten dimensions science speaks about in their Super String theory.

According to the Sefer Yetzirah, one of the primary books of the Kabbalah mentioned earlier, the Lord God of Hosts created and shaped the universe using ten numbers and the 22 letters of the Hebrew alphabet. He thus formed all things that are formed.

In order to create Light and sharing, the Vessel needed this darkness to work with. And so began our physical universe, where one percent of our reality also resides.

When God created the world, He knew that we, the vessels, could not receive His awesome blazing Light in Its totality. The Creator, in His infinite wisdom, therefore, concealed the greater portion of His Light, so as not to overwhelm that which He created.

Cayce said, "There is no difference between the unseen world and that which is visible; save that in the unseen, so much greater expanse or space may be covered." (5754-3)

Into a place of darkness, which is this world, we came.

We still had our remembrance of the Real World, or spiritual Endless World, where we originated from.

As time passed here on Earth, and after much experimenting within the mineral, plant, vegetable, and animal kingdoms, we started to lose our connection to the Light.

We forgot about our Creator and our true identity.

Our souls took on a physical body and an additional thought system of survival in order to maintain our existence here.

This was the beginning of our suffering, pain and misery which was absent in the Endless World, our true home.

We actually got stuck here on Earth and we have been trying to awaken and free ourselves ever since.

The Zohar says that the perpetual pull and tug of the material world is of such a magnitude, we forget our true purpose in life, to become more God-like, as we succumb to the illusions of physical existence.

Kabbalah teaches that we are here to lift the ten curtains of forgetfulness through proactive behavior, using resistance against the ego, and to reconnect with the Light of the Creator by transforming more of ourselves into Light.

According to the Cayce readings, the purpose of life is soul or spiritual growth. "The coming into the earth has been and is, for the evolution or the evolving of the soul unto its awareness." (5749-5)

Our Split Mind

Everything in this material world seems so real. Our bodies seem real. Our jobs seem real. Our homes and apartments seem real. Our possessions seem real, including our expensive cars, clothing, jewelry and money,

But are they?

The Kabbalistic statement, "That which is above is like unto that which is below," is true,

This world, and all of its appearances, are only a mere reflection of the Real World.

Once we know this is true within our hearts and minds, we will start to free ourselves from all of our problems.

The Cayce readings say, "All one sees manifest in a material world is but a reflection or shadow of the real or spiritual life." (262-23)

The first step in getting to know the truth is learning to identify the two parts of our mind.

We originally came here to earth with our God-like spirit consciousness. This was of the Light and so awesome. We were one with our Creator.

While in the body, however, we started thinking more and more with another thought system that is of a selfish nature. This became, and still is, the problem.

The Kabbalists refer to this other thought system as our Ego, or the opponent. It can trick us in a heartbeat. It can have us believe anything. All for self. So slick and so seemingly real and true. But a true deceiver! Some of the most intellectual, spiritual and good-hearted people have fallen prey to this false self.

The following Cayce reading confirms the ego's agenda. "Self glory, self-exaltation, self indulgence becometh those influences that become as abominations to the Divinity in each soul; and separate from a knowledge of Him." (1293-1)

In our lives we have to challenge this opponent or the evil inclination as it is called by the ancient Kabbalists. Our temptations are here by God design. We attract the very situations and people that draw out our shadow side to translate it into Light.

However, there is an upside and purpose to all of this struggle. It does make our soul strong and it helps us to get those dark curtains lifted, bringing in more Light and remembrance of who we really are.

I can recall the very first time I had recognized that there were two thought systems occupying my mind.

Many years ago, I was living in a high-rise apartment building in Manhattan Beach in Brooklyn, overlooking the Atlantic Ocean. It was early in the day and I was looking out the large picture window onto the beach and the ocean. Being winter, the temperature outside must have been about twenty degrees. Out of the blue, I heard an abrupt voice in my head say, "Why don't you go out there in the ocean for a swim?"

I couldn't believe it. It was insane! Why would I want to do that?

I then realized the temporary insanity of my ego mind. The opponent exposed itself to me on that day and changed my life ever since. It was so blatant that it blew its cover.

Sometimes we get to perceive our ego mind and sometimes we don't. It usually is very crafty, but on that day I caught on.

When we start to learn what is true and what is not, life begins to get a lot easier. More joy, love, peace and freedom are ours each time, through resistance, we choose the Light. Needless to say, I chose to stay dry.

Cayce spoke about truth in this reading, "Wherever Truth is made manifest it gives place to that which is heaven for those that seek and love truth." (262-87)

Kabbalist Rabbi Yehuda Ashlag, the 20th century mystic, said that people usually perceive events to be exactly opposite of their true state of reality because of their limited view of reality.

I think the opponent is the culprit the Rabbi is referring to, the ego self, who at times can easily mislead us and distort our perceptions. That is why we need to learn to be vigilant in order to avoid chaos and destructive influences in our lives.

How to Detect the Opponent

Recognition of the opponent and the negative traits he (using male terminology for both male and female) tries to instill in us is very important to self-transformation.

When you get angry in any way, he is there. When you feel jealous, he is there.

When you are doubtful or fearful over anything, he is there.

When you are pessimistic, he is there. Keep your eyes open, there is more. When you feel uncertain, he is there.

When you start to feel anxiety, he is there.

When you are insecure or overconfident, he is there.

When you know you shouldn't be doing something and you hear, "Go on and do it!" that's him.

As well as when you know you should be doing something, it is him who talks you out of it by saying, "Don't bother."

These are just the basics of how the opponent shows up in our lives. The fundamental law governing the universe and world is that of opposites.

There is no stability in the universe.

There is only movement.

We are either heading toward the Light or moving into darkness. It is our thoughts, our words, and our actions that determine our direction.

The opponent's job is to keep us from revealing more of the Light. He wants to diminish you and keep you small, feeling insignificant, keeping you in the dark. Our job is to bring more Light by lifting the curtains of darkness.

How else can we know when the opponent has taken control over our thought system?

When we deliberately look to hurt someone, know for sure at that moment, the opponent is in charge of our thoughts. By cheating or lying to another, there again is a red flag.

All of the negative "me first" thoughts, words and moves we make are ruled by the opponent urging us on.

When we buy the lie, we lose.

We lose our peace, our joy, and our harmony with ourselves and with others. We lose our awareness of the Light, which is what we are all looking for in the first place.

How do we know if we are being selfish, separate, and non-caring?

One of the clues is by what comes back to us.

The universe is a great messenger for letting us know if we are on the beam or not with right attitudes, thoughts and actions. What you sow is what you reap.

Cayce had some simple wisdom about this, "What ye do to others, ye are doing to thyself." (3198-3)

Our Mirrors

In any relationship, personal or business, people are good mirrors for us to see ourselves. They will show us in some way whether we are sharing the Light with them or being selfish. The quickest way for a person to lose his audience is to talk continuously about himself.

The opponent within us uses all relationships to strengthen us. *To remember that we are the Light is challenging, yet so important to our well-being.*

17

People are our best teachers. They test us to stay on course.

Children in particular have a way of testing us even more. When we're tired and a child wants to play with us, it is so easy to just say, "No." To give of ourselves is most important.

We can easily tell by a child's response if we are being selfish or not. Ignoring our children by excessively talking on the phone, or constantly focusing on other hand held electronic devices, can have an adverse effect on them as well, especially during mealtime or while driving. Much of our 24/7 technology are ego distractions.

We all are subject to negative thoughts and traits, but it is in our overcoming, using resistance, that we will be truly successful and happy. All those negative thoughts and traits are not even ours. They come from the opponent within. The untrue self.

Kabbalah says our remembrance of our Oneness with God and each other is the key.

Although we do appear as separate individuals, having separate bodies and thoughts, the truth is that *We Are One.* We are one with each other whether we like it or not, and we are one with God. We are Spirit and not our bodies. We live in and through our bodies. This truth can give us great leverage over the opponent who is demanding us to be separate, unloving, mildly miserable, and body focused.

Sometimes a big battle goes on in our minds between the opponent and the Light.

The opponent always speaks loud and usually first. The Light is that still small voice of intuition that speaks the truth. The opponent demands, while the Light requests and has a preference.

Each time we make a decision from the Light side of our being we feel peace. Each decision made by listening to the ego, or opponent, brings us chaos. It is that simple. But words are simple and actions are more difficult. Resistance.

Good News

The good news is that even when we make mistakes, it is only an indication that we need to learn something we didn't know. *We will always get a chance to do it again until we get it right, one way or another.*

Life is a classroom where there are needed lessons to be learned. What we sometimes call failure, God calls an unlearned lesson.

There is a difference. One is an evaluation coming from the opponent, giving us a negative feeling. The other is a statement that is constructive, coming from our loving Creator.

Which part of our mind we listen to will always determine our state of mind and emotions. *We have a choice.* All of this testing, which we actually do to ourselves, gives us opportunities to grow in spirit and earn more Light.

Our good friend Joni, a numerologist who also studies and practices Kabbalah, got a $150 parking ticket while making a clothing donation at a nursing home. She had parked her car at a bus stop to unload her items. A policewoman saw her, listened to her story, and still wrote up the ticket. At first Joni's ego kicked in. She couldn't believe that while making a donation she would get a ticket!

Then she had her miracle. Within minutes, she changed her mind from being upset to being at peace, recognizing her ego was offended at not being acknowledged for doing a good deed. The ticket was valid. She was parked at a bus stop. She decided to accept what is and see the money for the parking ticket as a donation to the city. Shortly thereafter, a letter was sent on her behalf to the court judge from one of the nursing administrators where she had made her donation, and her ticket was reduced to one hundred dollars. In addition, her numerology business soon increased significantly. The Light always works in wondrous ways.

Facing Our Problems Head On

The first step in problem solving is to remember *the problem is never the problem. It's our reaction to the problem that is the problem.*

This can't be emphasized often enough.

To help solve any problem, we need to try to realize deep within that we have everything we need to be happy now. We are spiritual beings. All of our problems are body related.

As spiritual beings we are lacking nothing. This means getting in touch with our true God-Self.

Kabbalah teaches us to not run away from our problems, but to meet them head on. It is only when we identify and transform our negative traits that more Light comes.

Cayce said, "Through trials, trouble, tribulations, one arrives at the best things in life and the trials are forgotten." (288-17)

I've learned that taking a position of a positive attitude through it all is important. Some positive thoughts like: "I can hardly wait to see the good that will come from this," can help.

Know that your problem has already been solved on the inner plane, the 99 percent realm, and success is yours forthcoming here in our one percent reality.

It is the trusting in this truth that helps to bring about the Light's Presence and the right solution. Any fear that enters your mind acts as a roadblock to the Light getting through. *Focusing on the Light is the key to eliminating fear.*

Letting Go

There are usually two basic types of problems, or emotional conflicts:

--Not getting what we want.

--Getting what we don't want.

Kabbalah says great peace occurs when we can let go of our attachments to all desires and just be.

Although it is a task to get above the ego self and let go, it has to be done and can be accomplished. We need a counter balance to work with, to realize that the Light of the Creator is always available within, and can be accessed at any time.

Problems, when properly perceived, can be used as great counter balances, showing us our weaknesses and helping us to become more centered in spirit.

Because we test ourselves with problems, we grow in the Light to rise above this world of illusion. When we do the internal work, then the external catalyst is gone. When something is no longer useful, it is discarded.

Rise above the problem first in your mind (ask the Light for help), and then the problem will be removed.

This is the reverse of how we usually think about being happy. We say, "Take this problem away and then I will be happy."

Again, the problem will only go away when we show that we can rise above it as if it never existed. It will then no longer be needed.

Problems can also be perceived as agents that provide opportunities to help us grow. They are not meant to make us suffer. We do that to ourselves.

Problems show us what part of our mind needs healing. What part is in fear of some kind. Once that part is healed, the problem will vanish. This simple truth has brought me great peace.

Remember, the mind cannot serve two masters. You are listening to the lower mind, the ego, when negativity and fear surface.

You are hearing the Voice of the Light from the Creator when positive peaceful thoughts surface.

Those negative thoughts are not the truth. They sometimes appear to be true, but all negative thoughts are a lie so *don't believe everything you think.*

People sometimes ask, "How do you know when you are hearing the Voice of the Light of the Creator?"

For me, it is what I call a "welling up" of new energy inside my mind and body.

The adrenal glands get activated as well. You start to feel stronger in your conviction of what you know you need to do. The Light's presence helps you to go forward with more assuredness. It is almost as if a strong wind comes and moves you quickly along.

There is also a wonderful peace that washes over you that you hadn't felt before. That's a sure sign of the Light's Presence. *Keeping quiet and still while waiting to hear from the Light is very important.*

Allow this welling up to occur in your mind by staying positive and certain. You will hear the still inner voice at the "right time."

Have patience. Never doubt that the Light of the Creator will come. Let the Light comfort you. Just ask. The Light will remove all of the chaos from our lives.

Kabbalah says that the more we can attune ourselves to the Light, the happier we will become. Overcoming ourselves is a deliberate process that requires constant discipline.

We are at our weakest when tired or frustrated. At these times it gets even more difficult to push through the opposition the opponent sets up for us. It seems like the ego knows exactly when we are most vulnerable. We become more confused, uncertain and susceptible to problems presenting themselves at those times. Our mental and emotional stability weaken and we sometimes fall. How important it is to keep focusing on the Light. It is our strength in times of challenges.

Simon Says

While working in the music business I got a phone call one day from my dear mother. She was always thinking of how to promote my music and had come up with a novel idea. This was back in the early 70's during the energy crisis and long gas lines. My hit song, *Simon Says,* was now a few years old. The name of the energy czar in Washington, D.C. was William Simon, Secretary of the Department of Energy.

Mom suggested, "Elliot, why don't you re-write the *Simon Says* lyrics relating it to William Simon and the energy crisis? It sounded like she may have been on to something. I told her I would think about it.

The next day inspiration came with new lyrics entitled, *SAVE OUR ENERGY (That's What Simon Says)*. At that time I also had my own record company, and one of the groups signed to the label was The Magid Triplets. They were identical brothers, a seasoned pop song and dance act. Dennis, Michael and Eddie were also friends of mine. I told them about the song and they were excited to record it. We went into the studio and within a short time the record was produced. After changing the group's name to The Energizers (for commercial purposes), the records were pressed and released.

I contacted William Simon's secretary in Washington D.C. and sent him a copy asking if the group and I could present it to Simon at his office as a promo event. In a few days he got back to me. It was a go. We would be at their next press conference in D.C.

My attorney at the time was Jerry Berger, who was also the attorney for King Features Syndicate. He planned to send their film crew to cover the event. Things were moving very quickly. When The Energizers and I got to the hotel in D.C., I called Simon's secretary to verify the time and place.

My ego got busted when I heard there was no time slot available for us to do the presentation. I was told to call back in 30 minutes. It had been a long drive down from New York City. I felt disappointed, but I didn't want to upset the group. During that half hour I chose to keep silent, unconsciously practicing behavioral Kabbalah. I kept my cool and didn't react.

When I called back I was told that although there was not enough time for us to attend the press conference, we would be able to meet Simon in his private office afterwards. I then told the group. At least we would get to see him and present the record.

When we got to Simon's office, the King Features' film crew was already set up, lights and all. Reporters from the press conference started coming in to see what was going on.

Before we knew it, we had our own press conference, and I made the presentation to Secretary Simon. The next day, the three major TV news networks, NBC, ABC and CBS were in the little Brooklyn recording studio where we recorded the song, covering the story. That night it was aired on all three stations. The day after, the news syndicates UPI and AP picked it up in print as well, with pictures of The Energizers. It was amazing!

Although the record was never a hit, we did manage to get some radio airplay. The lesson here was non-attachment to the outcome, and staying centered no matter what. Accepting what is.

Helping Others

The Cayce readings advise another good remedy for problem solving. "Helping others is the best way to rid yourself of your own troubles."(5081-1) "The joy, the peace, the happiness that may be ours is in doing for the other fellow." (262-3)

Personally, one way I've found that moves me into a higher state of mind, is the joy of playing the piano at retirement homes. Seeing them smile as they clap their hands and tap their feet to the music always boosts my spirit.

Each time we can help someone is a golden opportunity to share and receive more Light. It not only helps them but it also helps us at the same time. This is a universal law that never fails. As you give, you receive. Because we are one, this law is infallible.

We can help someone by listening or simply showing up when needed. That is the Light coming in. There is a never-ending supply that is always available to us from the Creator. All we need to do is remember to call upon the Light.

Judge Not

Many years ago while working as a new car salesman for an Oldsmobile dealership, I obviously needed to learn a lesson about non-judgment.

A shabbily dressed man walked into the showroom looking at the latest models. There was a sales rotation system so each salesman would get a fair chance to sell. It was my turn when this customer walked in. My ego immediately judged this man as not being able to afford a new car. Thinking it was a waste of time, I turned the customer over to a salesman friend.

As it turned out, the man I poorly judged bought a new car. My friend earned a nice commission and I learned a valuable lesson. That old saying, "Never judge a book by its cover," is so true.

The ego thinks it knows everything when in fact the opposite is true. Judging ourselves also has a negative effect on our behavior. Sometimes we think we are less than, or greater than our neighbor. We lose sight of the fact that we are all on this journey together to remember we are the Light.

The ego likes to compare ourselves to others, for good or bad. No one is greater. No one is lesser. We are all equal sparks of that Divine Light, doing our best in our own way.

Dumping Our Stuff

The Light wants to reveal itself like never before. In today's world, there is a lot of stress and pain going on in just about all of our lives. We are in the process of dumping much of our old garbage that is holding us back.

Now that we are in the new millennium, higher vibrational frequencies of Light are being sent down rapidly for us to absorb and incorporate in all of our cells as the earth is speeding up. Much of the fear we have been hiding deep inside is being revealed so that it can be removed to bring in more of the Light.

Being aware of what is happening on a cosmic level, we can take some kind of action to reduce the growing pains. One of the most effective ways to clear ourselves quickly of any pressure, is to become more aware of being both the observer and participant of our lives, rather than just the participant. We are innately the participants all of the time. The good news is that we are more than our physical bodies. We are spirit. We are Light.

I remember being in the Army Reserve in my early twenties, training to be a personnel specialist in the Signal Corps. During a typing class, a practice phrase to be typed repeatedly was: "To know and to know that you know is a good thing." I kept this message in my wallet for many years to come. True wisdom is practical use of knowledge. I've learned with knowledge of spirit comes understanding and peace.

Remember, according to the Kabbalah, the physical body is *only one percent of our true essence.*

The other 99 percent is our spirit essence, which we are not always fully aware of.

Knowing this can take the sting out of many irritating situations.

By remembering to be the observer as well as the participant of this one percent reality, we can stay centered as we get pulled and tugged in this chaotic world with its many distractions. If we remember the Light, we can give thanks for any condition we encounter and know it will eventually be in our best interest. Non-reaction is the key.

The Love Connection

Because obstacles are opportunities to connect to the Light, they help us remove the curtains blocking the Light. Some of the other obstacles the ego presents play out in fear, guilt, anger, envy, lust, possessiveness, greed, arrogance and self-pity. These emotions can come up at different times and take over our thought system.

Each time we overcome any of these negative emotions, we bring in more Light.

In fact, Kabbalah says the bigger the obstacle, the more potential Light! If we can remember Love opens all the doors to understanding, we will connect with the Light more easily.

Cayce confirms: "…as the progress is made, as the understanding comes more and more, never, NEVER does it make the manifested individual entity other than the more humble, the more meek, the more long suffering, the more patient. Of this ye may be sure." (281-31)

There is a great need to dwell continually upon the Love of God, to look into the Light and recognize His goodness is always working through us, no matter what is going on. Honestly looking back over our lives, we can see the growth from each experience. When we choose to do this, and ask the Light to help us, we can overpower our negative

31

inclinations. By doing so, we will stay connected and see the Light. It will manifest in many ways here on Earth. Inner peace will be our constant companion as we experience the Real World.

Chapter 3

WE ARE THE LIGHT

Kabbalah reminds us of the answers to those age-old questions. Who are we? Why are we here? Where did we come from? And, where are we going?

The Light is the answer to all of these questions.

We are the Light. We will always be the Light. Of this we can be sure no matter how dark things may look. The Light is. It is where we came from and where we are returning to. There is Light in everything and everyone.

Kabbalah teaches that each of us is born with a unique role and ability to enhance the world.

We have within us all the power and glory of our Creator to do wonderful things and overcome all obstacles. Be in awe of the Light and how it tries to talk to us through everything around us. Since the

Light is in and around us always, the work to be done is to remove the veils that block out the Light.

Cayce's wisdom says, "Know that the purpose for which each soul enters a material experience is that it may be as a light unto others." (641-6)

He also stated, "That we may make manifest the love of God and man." (254-42)

When we look around the world and our home town too, we can see many man-made accomplishments that greatly reflect the Light of the Creator. Numerous artists and musicians as well as architects and athletes have contributed to this grand outpouring of Light. Sometimes athletes call this "being in the zone." Within a higher reality it is actually connecting with the Creator's Light.

Looking at the Great Pyramid in Egypt, you can see how awesome the Light truly is. During the Renaissance period there was a great dispensation of Light coming through the arts, leaving a legacy of magnificent creativity that has continued to uplift humanity to this present day. We use the term inspired works when describing many of these great masterpieces.

In Webster's dictionary, the word *inspire* means to breathe--more at spirit. There is so much potential within each of us because of the Light.

To remember that we are unlimited human beings because of our heritage, can truly help us.

I've found it important to *ask to be a channel for the Light*. When you are a willing channel and connect to the Light of the Creator, you will be more quickly put in the right place at the right time.

This is because we are attuning to a cosmic power that connects us to the 99 percent reality. Being a channel for the Light means being open for and to everything. It means admitting we don't know how to solve our own problems, but we are willing to be shown.

As unlimited Light-beings, we also have that same power of creation to co-create more of our divine nature.

We can literally rise above every weakness we have to become better at who we are. Kabbalah is all about growing. No matter what level we're at, there is always a need to come up higher. The challenge is to avoid getting stuck in complacency, our comfort zone.

We can stop bad habits and old programming if we put out our intention of will to do so. Our will is connected to the Light of the Creator.

Cayce had this to say about the power of our will. "The will of the soul attuned to God may change the circumstances or the environment...in fact, all the forces even in nature itself." (3374-1)

When confronted with a problem or a conflict in a relationship, get excited about the Light that person is trying to give you on a hidden level. Know this secret. Be aware that the Light of the Creator is in that person, too.

There is literally nothing that cannot be accomplished if it is in alignment with the Creator's will. To the degree we are able to transform our negative nature, that is the measure of hidden Light that will be revealed in our lives. The bigger the problem, the greater the opportunity for more Light. We can rise as high as we fall.

Lightworking

I have noticed how much practicing the Kabbalah principles has helped me transform during periods of money challenges.

Working in the creative arts field can be financially uncertain at times. There are windfalls and then there are those valleys that can really be challenging. I know, according to Kabbalah, challenges help us, but speaking now from an emotional "street level," here's another story:

A music publisher, who had not been paying my writer royalties on time, was again late with royalty payments. In the past when I called him, needing the money owed, my ego would flare up and get somewhat abrupt. I would lose my cool, and in reality, lose my connection to the Light of God consciousness. It would happen almost automatically. Even though there was just cause to confront him, it was done in the old fearful negative reactive way.

Because I've learned the Light's way (to first call upon the Light of the Creator), when I recently called that same publisher (again needing the money owed) about overdue royalties, I felt an immediate shift in my awareness. I was coming from my soul and not my ego. It was amazing that I kept positive thoughts about this man even though my ego was dissatisfied with the situation.

I took it a step further remembering that the publisher and the money owed to me were not my true salvation. In that moment of transformation, I realized God was in charge. And all was well with my soul, no matter what. I was genuinely at peace. I actually did become the observer and not just the participant.

As it turned out, the Light's approach did prevail and I received my check soon thereafter. More importantly, I recognized my soul's growth. I was no longer coming from fear, which a lack of money can bring up.

When we call upon the Light to help us control our negative emotional ego mind, the Light will come and transform us, bring us peace and produce the right results.

When we get to the point of self-awareness that we are not just our physical bodies but actual Light-beings, we start to act and see things

37

differently. We become more masterful in many ways that happen naturally as part of our transformed nature.

Cayce had this good advice on problem solving. "Meet the problems first, though, in the spiritual; then the mental and the material results will become more satisfactory." (459-12)

The Power of Sound

More power is given to us from the Light as we prove we can handle it. The more self-control we can master, the more Light is made available for us to share.

Some of our vocabulary changes, and there is a higher percentage of positive words that come to our mind. I've started using more non-reactive words like, "Whatever" and "So?" and "Oh, well," to help diffuse many situations. Loving thoughts and kind right speech increase the Light quotient within ourselves, the people around us, and our planet.

Many people don't realize that everything has a vibrational frequency, including thoughts and words. The more positive the outpouring, the more it will come back to you.

The more negative the outpouring, the same holds true. We have a choice at every given moment to be more God-like. This choice helps to create our reality here in the physical world.

The Zohar says, "Words are vessels that draw particular blends of energy into our lives. Human speech possesses power that can directly influence the world around us. Hence, we should take great care in choosing what we say."

The Zohar also encourages us to use our speech for spiritual purposes, so that our words inspire Light in others instead of adding darkness to the world.

Cayce advised, "...don't get mad and don't cuss a body out mentally or in voice. This brings more poisons than may be created by even taking foods that aren't good."(470-37) "Do not hold resentment. Do not get so mad at times when things are a little wrong. Remember that others have as much right to their opinions as self, but that there *is* a level from which all may work together for good. Smile always—and *live* the smile!" (1819-1)

Constantly connecting to the 99 percent realm is the key to happiness and is a necessity on the path of higher evolution.

Whenever we want help in attracting the right opportunities and the right people in our lives, we need to connect with the Light. When we want stronger and more loving relationships, we need the Light. Whenever we desire more hope, enthusiasm, and self-motivation for any challenge, the Light is the answer. Keep on asking to be a channel for the Light. *Remember that persistent self-effort on a daily basis is the key. It is not just knowing what to do, but actually doing it, that will make the difference in your life. The negative ego gets lazy. You may need to push a little harder.*

Music is the Bridge

Whenever writing music or lyrics I always ask to be connected to the Light of the Creator. When I do this, the songs can become portals of more Light for everyone, as well as the planet itself. Keeping positive-minded helps to do this. This is true for all creative endeavors.

Several years back a request came to me from a visually challenged student at the Cayce/Reilly Massotherapy School. She was told to listen to music played in three different keys, A, C-sharp and B-flat, to help promote the healing of her vision. Knowing that I play the keyboard, she asked if I could write and record music for her in those particular keys. I agreed to help and gift her with the music. The only problem was that although I can write music, I play by ear, mostly in the key of C, no sharps or flats.

Because I made this commitment, I asked the Light for help and an amazing thing happened.

That night I sat down at the keyboard, affirmed absolute certainty, and within an hour I had composed and recorded two of the songs. Early the next morning, the Light sent in the third song. All written in the keys she had requested. It was remarkable!

Not only was I able to help someone, but was given three gifts of wonderful music to add to my catalog. *As Kabbalah teaches, it is in your sharing that you receive.* This was a miracle and I knew it.

Color and sound can be used to release tremendous positive energy if we act more like the Light in using them for our creations. The more positive the creation, the more Light is able to be sent out. How wonderful it would be if more and more artists, filmmakers and musicians would remember this. The energy of the people and the planet could be positively transformed in a short period of time.

The Cayce readings stress the importance of filling our souls with music. "Do learn music. It is part of the beauty of the spirit. For remember, music alone may span that space between the finite and the infinite." (3659-1)

In another reading, he stressed the influence of music in the cosmos. "Music, color, vibration are all a part of the planets, just as the planets are a part -- and a pattern-- of the universe." (5755-1)

The readings also tell us that we can actually heal by using sound and color. "Sounds, music, and color may have much to do with creating the proper vibrations about individuals that are mentally unbalanced, physically deficient or ill in body and mind." (1334-1)

Being a musician, I have witnessed the miraculous effects of music on the soul. In September of 2002, when my mother was suffering from cancer, our family gathered around her bedside during the last days of her life. We sang joyful songs to her. At times I also brought in the keyboard and played for her, to help ease the pain. The soft melodies lulled her back to sleep in but a few minutes. I knew she was listening. My heart felt at peace.

According to Cayce, whenever we find ourselves in need of a mood lift, a shift can happen just by using our voice. "Then, sing a lot about the work—in everything the body does. Hum, sing—to self; not to be heard by others but to be heard by self."(3386-1)

"And whenever there are the periods of depression, or the feeling low or forsaken, play music; especially stringed instruments of every nature. These will enable the entity to span that gulf as between pessimism and optimism." (1804-1)

Music can also be helpful in the decision-making process. In one reading, Cayce advised the client, "If there arises in the experience, then, a decision to be made, whether upon the material things, a change in residence, a change of environments of any nature or type, do so under the influence of such music."(1042-2) The such music referred to in this reading related to soft natural sounds. Finer types of music develop our higher selves.

Cayce had more to say about singing, "Hence as ye gain in the outpouring of thyself in song, ye not ONLY give praise and service and obedience but bring help and hope, and an awakening to those ye contact IN the very act." (1158-14)

The Zohar affirms: Through singing, Light is drawn.

Living a Balanced Life

We must also assert ourselves in controlling our body. The opponent is just waiting for a little opening, to break in and steal our real joy.

All of the over-indulgences of our physical body are a clue the opponent is trying to take away our power. We do need to be strong against any of these temptations in order to stay balanced.

Cayce explains, "Through diet and exercise the greater portion of all disturbances may be equalized and overcome, if the right mental attitude is kept."(288-38)

Moderation in all things is an important key to remember as well. The Cayce readings advise, "Keep a normal balance, not being an extremist in any direction,--whether in diet, exercise, spirituality or morality,--but in all let there be a coordinant influence. For every phase of the physical, mental, and spiritual life is dependent upon the other. They are one." (2533-3) "Do not be excessive in anything! Do not be abnormal! Let's be normal in everything!" (340-29) "Work as well as you play, and play as well as you work." (279-2)

Our friend, Peter Van Daam, has put together a wonderful simple daily exercise program based on the Edgar Cayce Readings. I have been doing them for over eight years and can feel a positive difference in my energy levels and overall health (See additional resources in back of book).

Heart Thinking

"Let thy disappointments and sorrows take wings. Let love and hope remain with thee."
Edgar Cayce Reading (281-40)

The seat of our soul is in our heart. Also in our heart is where the Divine spark of the Creator dwells. Sometimes we may find it difficult to remember this, but when we do, peace is always restored.

In this time of major transition, we are being asked to think from our heart first. This is a major shift from cerebral thinking first.

When we think with our heart, love is being generated into our minds and our words. People respond more positively when we are heart and soul oriented. No one feels threatened or attacked when love rules.

The practice of heart thinking is the keynote of this wonderful new age we are living in. We do it some of the time, but we can do it all of the time when we "see our brother as our self." We truly are one, and that thought can keep us heart-centered. If we put God first in every situation, we will Light it up. Remembering this will help to keep us centered.

Cayce cautions us to remain vigilant to the Creator in times of challenge. "Watch, that ye be not overcome. Watch and pray, for as the Father giveth so does the understanding come as to what may be accomplished in the efforts of the self in relationships to others; and ye are the light-bearers for Him." (262-26)

It is also important to try to remain above the clouds. It is easy to be cheerful when there are cheerful people around and all is going well. The same is true for being loving and kind. When people around us are loving and kind, it makes it a whole lot easier to be that way as well. But when darkness comes it is more challenging. When there is tension in the room and scowls start appearing on people's faces, how well do we do then?

Remember, these are the tests that the opponent throws at us, with our permission at a higher level, in order to grow. Remaining true to the Light, as radiant beings, is what is always called for;

45

not falling for the physical appearances. They come and go, but the Light is always constant.

As stated in the Cayce readings, "Let thy light so shine unto others that they may see the way." (281-50)

It's About Time

From a vantage point of looking into our one percent realm from the 99 percent realm, we can see that time is really man-made and doesn't exist. Time appears to exist to our five senses. But from a spiritual point of view, time is an illusion.

Kabbalah calls time the distance between good deeds and their dividends or between cause and effect. The opponent sometimes is able to use time against us through delays to thwart our success. Know that we are being tested during those periods and that we need to be strong and certain that the Light will come.

Although we work through time in this dimension, it must not be allowed to control our lives. Yesterday may contain thoughts of past guilt (ego thoughts), which must be dismissed for more Light to come.

Tomorrow thoughts also need to be held in abeyance, or we may fill ourselves with anxiety.

Today, which is the only time there is, is a composite of all three time factors. Our opponent, who knows this so well, will tempt us into procrastinating in the now. It does this by presenting challenges that cause us to postpone timely constructive actions. *We must stay vigilant for living in the now. It is our power point for eternity.*

"LIVIN' IN THE NOW"

We're Livin' In The Now
We're happy as can be
We're Livin' In The Now
With joy in our hearts
Filled with peace filled with harmony

We're Livin' In The Now
Tomorrow's here today
We're Livin' In The Now
Forget all the past
All the thoughts that we once did say

Now is the time we are talkin' about
I said that now is the time
We just can't live without
You know that now is the time
Now it's eternity
Remember first who you are
You can set yourself free

Words and Music by Elliot Chiprut

47

According to the Cayce readings on time, there is only the present. "Hence we find visions of the past, visions of the present, visions of the future. For to the subconscious there is no past or future—all present. This would be well to remember." (136-54)

All of our past has brought us to our *now* point. The truth is, the past is over, and only the good is what remains. All of the so-called bad or difficult experiences were only stumbling blocks being turned into stepping-stones, making us better along the way.

The following quotation from Cayce emphasizes this point when asked, "Was the experience I have gone through necessary?"

The answer was, "Unless the entity, unless the body looks upon the experiences day by day as necessary influences and forces, and uses them as a stepping-stone, soon does life become a pessimistic outlook. If each and every disappointment, each and every condition that arises, is used as a stepping-stone for better things and looking for and expecting it, then there will still be continued the optimism. Or the looking for and the expecting of. If an individual doesn't expect great things of God, he has a very poor God, hasn't he?" (462-10)

There is always major growth when a stumbling block appears on our path. Sometimes there is more than one block simultaneously, indicating that we have contracted on some level of our being, an acceleration in our spiritual development.

The higher part of our mind, or spirit part, knows this to be true. The lower part, or ego, usually takes objection to the opposition, judging it to be bad and reacts negatively. As we continue to rise in consciousness and self-awareness, we are able to react less and be more at peace.

This is the growth process in action.

Reaching *the peace that passes all understanding* is our goal. This is accessing the Kingdom of God within where Light and Love abide.

It is not an easy process, but one in which every human being is working on, whether he or she realizes it or not.

Everyone is allowed to make mistakes and correct them time and time again.

That is what time is for, to be used to get things right and in balance while we are in the physical body. When we have mastered ourselves, we can then be promoted to a higher ground.

Chapter 4

HUMAN DESIRE

Kabbalah uses the word "desire" as a definition of our essence, our driving force. Kabbalist Rabbi Yehuda Ashlag wrote: "Humans would not twitch a single finger if not for some inner desire, and that all desires originate as a pure intent to experience the Light Force of the Creator."

Some of these human desires that give us our separate identities are: intellectual, sexual, religious, material, enlightenment, travel, adventure, fame, power, and solitude.

Kabbalah also says that there is no limit to our desires, and our desire's primary objective is uninterrupted happiness.

By acting more like the Creator and reflecting the Light through sharing and caring, we can create miracles, fulfilling our desires.

Miracles do not come from this physical one percent limited world, although we activate them from here.

They come from the 99 percent realm, or Tree of Life reality. Thinking of the grandeur of the Creator allows us to leave this one percent realm and enter into the Endless World of miracles.

The Creator always wants us to have miracles. We block them by our uncertainty that they exist, or we can access them, or that we even deserve them. If we don't share our Light, miracles will not occur.

These basic truths will help us manifest our desires. *The inner work on self, through self-discipline, is the key to unlocking miracles.*

Again, we create the miracles by becoming a channel for the Light. This is the Kabbalist's secret. The Endless World, or Tree of Life reality, contains everything we desire. Nothing is too big or too difficult for the Light. In our commitment to the truth our miracles will be seen.

According to the Cayce readings, "What separated spirit from its first cause or causes good and evil? Desire! Desire! Hence desire is the opposite of will. Will and desire, one with the Creative Forces of Good, brings all its influence in the realm of activity that makes for that which is constructive." (5752-3)

The question, "Where does desire originate?" was posed to the sleeping Cayce. His answer was "will." (262-62) "Will and desire are spiritual as well as carnal as well as mental." (315-3)

The one major problem about desire the Kabbalists reveal, is *the human desire to receive for the self alone.*

When we do this, we disconnect from the Light and discontent eventually sets in.

All desire, directed by wisdom, carries a blessing for us and the rest of creation as it goes forth with the feeling of love.

Years ago, I had written an inspirational song called, *Lord Look Down On Me.* One of the lines in the song referring to desire went like this: "Lose your desire and put out the fire, it will come your way."

Unfulfilled desires cause us to be unhappy in many ways. We need to be alert to discern our desires. Are they guided by wisdom from our higher self? Or are they misguided desires from our selfish ego?

Changing Our Desires to Preferences

Have you ever noticed your emotions when the things in life that you desire start to move in your direction? You get a happy, uplifting feeling that all is well and that perhaps God is smiling down on you. This is a very natural feeling.

The question now is, is there a way to still be happy when the things we desire are withheld?

Through my experience, I know there is. *The mind set of being in the world, but not of it, is the key.* Again, by becoming both the observer and the participant will help us immensely.

The main focus, if we are vigilant enough, is to be on God, and not solely on any desire.

This is not to say that we don't have the desire for something, we are still human. But if we focus on God, Who is our supplier of all good, then we are not as subject to a "let down." It's about God acceptance.

Also, by *changing our desires to preferences,* helps to give us better emotional balance. God, in His infinite wisdom, has a perfect plan for all of us. Remember, He dwells within us and wants us to be happy always.

Sometimes it's difficult to see His perfection when things are withheld, but there are hidden blessings in all circumstances, both positive and negative ones. It does take faith and trust. However, when we acknowledge that God wants only good for us, miracles start to occur.

The first and most important miracle is our shift in perception that overrides this illusory world. We are more in control of our emotional body and we start to feel better, no matter what is going on in our life.

Instead of negatively dwelling on a withheld desire, we focus on God and His infinite wisdom.

The following inspirational thoughts can aid us in shifting our perception:

> *God is everywhere.*
> *God is guiding me.*
> *God is love.*
> *God is wisdom.*
> *God is truth.*

There is always a reason why, if our desire is being withheld. It doesn't matter if we can figure it out or not. Trust that there is a good reason for all things. God still loves us. Automatic pilot is a wonderful experience when we can let go and let God. True acceptance is the key.

Cayce points out, "That which is carnal and that which is mental and that which is spiritual may be found—in desire for, it builds – and is that which is the basis of evolution and of life and of truth. It also takes hold on hell and paves the way for many that find themselves oft therein." (262-60)

We are here on this planet as students in the school of life. There are always problems that will come up to be solved to help us grow and gain more Light.

If we can remember that everything we desire is really another form of Light from the Creator, from the 99 percent realm, we will start to adjust our thought process and look to connect more to the Light Source directly.

Staying True to Self

Kabbalah says that if we want true happiness, we need to get past our ego driven desires and embrace what our soul needs for upliftment and transformation.

Again, it is most important to connect with the Light, our secret key to Life's fulfillment. This alone will give us uninterrupted happiness.

This truth was pointed out to me early in my music career. In the late 1960's, by the age of 24, I was fortunate to have earned two gold records. Both pop records, *Little Bit O'Soul* by the Music Explosion, which I co-produced, and *Simon Says* (mentioned earlier) by the 1910 Fruitgum Co., which I wrote and co-produced, each sold over a million copies.

At that time, I was not on any spiritual path. Even though I was born into a Jewish family and had early religious training, I was not yet connecting with God and the Light. It was all about me and my ego. Soon after, even with my music career in full swing, the initial glow of material success faded. I was left with a feeling of emptiness inside. "Was this all there is to life?"

One night, out for a drive in my new Eldorado Cadillac, and brimming with material success, I was, for no visible reason, in deep pain and sadness. So much so, I slammed on the brakes in the middle of East 98th Street in Brooklyn, NY, near where I lived, and cried out, "God, please help me!"

From that moment on, something happened to me that changed my life.

I started to transform.

I was exhausted at being someone I was not. I just had to push past my ego's nature and get back into my true self.

God heard my prayer and an interesting thing soon occurred. To my shocking surprise, one night, the Cadillac was stolen off my driveway. The leasing company immediately replaced it. A few months later that Cadillac was also stolen off my driveway!

I then realized the expensive car no longer mattered. That was no longer who I thought I was. I went out and bought a new VW bug and I enjoyed it.

That was the beginning of getting free of my possessions *possessing* me. What liberation! It was truly a blessing in disguise. The Light was starting to show itself, and I was beginning to get free of my ego's stronghold.

Cayce advises not to get caught up in the material world. "Do not be over anxious about the material things. For the mental and the spiritual aspects and desires should be set in those directions where unto it may be said in the experience of self, 'I myself will be guided by the influences from the inner meditations, and that which is shown me from within.' For to such the promises are sure. If ye will seek this way, there may come those experiences that will not only be of more harmonious nature in the affairs in material things, but will bring that contentment which comes from knowing within self that the way is being kept that leads to a greater understanding in the truths, in mental experiences of a body." (681-1)

The receiving of a desire for self alone has many people wondering why they can't hold on to their contentment. The universal law works this way:

If we have a desire to receive something that we want to share, all is well. We will be content because there is a connection to the Light.

On the other hand, the desire to receive for self alone causes a quick burnout because it goes against the universal law. We lose the connection with the Light. There is no way to get around this truth.

Many wealthy people who live self-centered lives will not have inner peace for long. They will have the money in the bank, but not the lasting contentment they thought it would bring.

The same holds true in a self-centered relationship. They will have the partner but will not feel the heart-filled warmth of a loving relationship.

Any desire that is strictly ego driven for self alone will not satisfy us long term.

The Kabbalah's secret for receiving more Light which is what we are looking for in everything, is that *in our giving is our receiving.*

But we need to be careful not to give with an attitude of doing a favor for someone, expecting to receive, or that we are losing something by giving something up. This will cause a disconnect with the Light and we will not feel the blessing. We need to remember, we receive when we share, and to share when we receive. That is the gift from the Light.

Feeling the Shift

When following these principles we can actually feel a positive shift in our being. It works.

We start to feel lighter because more Light is coming to us from the Endless World. We become more like God. The Light connection is being made and we are the fortunate recipients.

Choosing our desires with a higher consciousness of oneness gives us peace. There is no burnout.

An alignment with the Will of the Creator is our key to much unending joy and true happiness.

Cayce deepens this thought. "So soon as man contemplates his free will he thinks of it as a means of doing the opposite of God's will, though he finds that only by doing God's will does he find happiness. Yet the notion of serving doesn't sit well with him, for he sees it as a sacrifice of his will. Only in disillusion and suffering, in time, space, and patience, does he come to the wisdom that his real will is the will of God, and its practice is happiness and heaven." (2537-1)

Kabbalah says unhappiness indicates a lack of fulfillment which stimulates a desire to receive for the self alone.

The opponent likes to tempt us with the desire for self alone. This can cause us great pain and misery if we are not aware that this temptation is coming from the opponent. He makes it all seem so right at the time.

The opponent may have others join in with our seeming right desire, looking as if they're adding to the rightness of it. However, if the group's desire is not in accordance with God's will, it will fail. Although sometimes it may temporarily manifest only to find out that it brought pain instead of gain. It doesn't matter if thousands of people have the same desire. If it is not in accordance with the Light of the Creator, it will not fulfill its purpose.

The rule to remember is, "One with God is a majority." The Light of God never fails.

The ego's desire of giving to get never works. The law of Truth and Light doesn't compromise. Even if we succeed at getting something through this incorrect intention, it will not bring lasting fulfillment and happiness. The Light eventually will always prevail.

Some good news about true desire from Cayce, "As creative activities are applied, what ye desire becomes law." (5265-1)

Kabbalah also teaches that our consciousness creates our reality. *Whatever we put our attention on is what we will receive. Think on the bright side.*

If we are projecting negative thoughts, that is what we will attract.

This is why it is very important to keep positive minded and stay focused on the Light and not on any results or outcomes. The 'how' will be shown to us by the Light at its proper time. This is the law of attraction.

One Cayce reading advised, "Thus the purpose of each experience is that the entity may magnify and glorify that which is good. For good is of the one source, God, and is eternal." (2599-1)

By magnifying the positive and minimizing the negative, we grow in grace, knowledge and understanding.

Kabbalah wants us to remember the Light will always give us what we need for our spiritual growth, not always what we want.

A well known Kabbalistic principle says, the more we seek to comprehend our purpose and the reality of the Creator, the more spiritual Light we receive.

This Cayce reading illustrates the importance of making the Earth a better place because you were here. "The purpose in life, then, is not the gratifying of appetites nor of any selfish desires, but it is that the entity, the soul, may make the earth, where the entity finds its consciousness, a better place in which to live." (4047-2)

Sex Awareness

Another important Kabbalistic truth says there is no more profound, potent, or potentially spiritual conduit for the expression of our desire than sex. However, as you can see by the size and growth of the pornography business around the globe, we need help.

We need more Light in this area than ever before. People don't realize what a huge trap this has become as the opponent is holding many people back from their true purpose on earth, to bring more Light.

Cayce says, "(Sex relations are) of the highest vibrations that are experienced in a material world...and are the basis of that which is termed the original sin; and hence may be easily misunderstood, misconstrued, misinterpreted, in the experience of **every** individual, but these would be known—that the control of such, rather than being controlled by such gives that which makes for the awareness of **spiritual** intent and purpose." (911-5)

In answer to this question asked of the sleeping Cayce, "How should love and sexual life properly function?" He answered, "...the relations in sexual life should be the outcome—not the purpose of, but the outcome of the answering of soul to soul in their associations... know that Love and God are One; that relations in the sexual life are the manifestations in the mental attributes of each so concerned. For, unless such associations become on such a basis, they become vile in the experience of those who join in such relations." (272-7)

In the Zohar we learn that "when a man and a woman join together in sexual union within the spiritual confines of marriage, their connection creates a stirring above: The Lower World embraces the Upper World and Divine Light fills all. But the man and woman must be pure of thought and joined by love. Their union must be accompanied by a consciousness to share pleasure for the purpose of creating Light for each other and the world."

Cayce also recommended sex education for the young, even before puberty, in the following reading. "Even in the **formative** years... even as the child studies its letters, let a portion of the instructions be in the care of the body, and more and more the stress upon the care in relation to the sex of the body. Do not begin after there has already begun the practice of the conditions that make for the destructive forces, or for the issue of the body itself— to become as a burning within the very elements of the body itself--and to find expression in the gratifying of the emotions." (826-6)

Remember this is a perfect universe, and if you are not currently engaged in an intimate sexual relationship, it only means for now those creative energies are being directed in other areas for your soul's growth.

Chapter 5

CERTAINTY IN TRUSTING GOD

The importance and purpose of this chapter is to help get us stronger in our conviction that the Light of God actually exists and that *there is nothing to fear*.

Fear is of the ego, or our untrue self.

Fear holds us back from enjoying everyday life and having great freedom.

Fear robs us of our peace, well being, and our true identity.

Kabbalah says that *absolute certainty* is our antidote for fear, which is a negative emotion.

Connecting with the Light banishes all fear. Trusting God removes all fear. We need to conquer our fears with love, not merely cope with them. This is easier said than done, but with the Light of God all things are possible. Cayce says, "Where there is real faith, there is no fear; for with faith in the abiding love of the Father, what cause is there ever for an anxious moment?" (262-18)

Whenever challenges appear and doubt sets in, we sometimes become uncertain of the power and reality of the Creator.

We begin to have fear thoughts and may even start blaming others.

These negative thoughts and feelings can be healed very quickly by injecting absolute certainty. Doubt actually pulls the plug from the Light source.

Certainty keeps the plug in.

It is important to resist uncertainty, for uncertainty only prolongs the chaos.

This Kabbalah secret is most helpful in our overcoming self, changing our nature, and bringing more Light. The Light's power is awesome and the opponent cannot win when absolute certainty is present. This is trust in action.

House-Sitting

During another financially challenging time, my wife Karen and I took up a friend's offer to house-sit in northern Virginia. At the end of our fifth month, we were ready to move on. But how? We had no visible resources. Our funds were still frozen at the credit union, but change was stirring in our hearts.

Early one evening we decided to go for a walk around a small lake in the area. As soon as we got out of the car, we noticed an unusual sight.

A blue heron was standing on the roof of the covered wooden foot bridge. Patiently, he stood motionless looking out over the lake for sustenance. Its long chest feathers fluttered in the breeze.

This was a first, as herons are usually seen wading in marshlands.

This one was definitely *out there*. It almost seemed like the heron wanted to get our attention. We smiled and took our walk.

When we returned thirty minutes later, to our surprise, it was still standing tall on the roof.

Only now it stood on one leg.

In his book, *Animal-Speak*, Ted Andrews teaches that heron symbolizes aggressive self-determination and self-reliance. Knowing God speaks to us through everything, the heron's obvious message was for us to step out in faith while we still had a leg to stand on.

The next week we did just that, moving back to Virginia Beach. We found a kitchenette at the Traveler's Inn motel, charged our rent, and focused on God.

During our third week there, we had a little money miracle with the credit union, when some of our funds became available. Shortly thereafter, a sunny, small two bedroom apartment appeared for rent in the newspaper. It was affordable and we grabbed it.

That whole experience taught us not to take anything for granted and to give thanks for everything that comes our way. Both the good and the seeming not so good.

Karen and I both have learned the importance of trusting God and being certain. Our financial challenges actually have helped to bring us closer to the Light of the Creator. We needed to stay positive, no matter what our bank account looked like.

We also needed to not blame each other, knowing that God had a greater plan for us. That what we were seeing with our five senses wasn't the truth. It took work, getting over the ego's fears of survival. By doing the spiritual work, applying the Kabbalah's principles, we were transformed positively in several areas of our lives.

We now feel more of the peace of God through this major transformation. It is a good indication we are well on the path to overcoming more of self, bringing in more Light, and accessing even greater freedom.

Cayce speaks of testing periods and certainty in God's promise, "Know that ye are going through a period of testing. Remain true to all that has been committed to thee, and know that each day is an opportunity and an experience. Speak a word for thy ideal. Not as to force an issue but ever constructive.

Sow the seed of truth, the seed of the spirit. God will give the increase." (3245-1)

Overcoming Fear

Sometimes when we enter a completely dark room, we can feel fearful. When we turn on the light, the fear goes away, changing our negative emotions to more positive feelings. Life works the same way. When we go into a situation that we are in the dark about, sometimes fear starts to creep in.

As soon as we discover what it is all about, and more Light is shed on the situation, we feel better. The fear of the unknown can paralyze us to a point of inaction. We can't go forward even though we may want to.

It helps to remember that the part of our mind thinking fear thoughts is not our true self.

Knowing that we are really one with the Light can shine away all fear thoughts. There can be no fear where there is Light. Again, the mind cannot serve two masters. It is impossible for the dark to live in the Light. When the Light is on, the dark, or the fear, vanishes. We must keep the Light on at all times to be happy.

Kabbalah teaches us how to do this. The secrets of the Light revealed in both Kabbalah and the Edgar Cayce Readings are a great gift to humanity from our Creator. Because we can learn to choose the

69

Light over the dark, we can choose to be happy. Our consciousness can dictate what we are feeling. This Kabbalistic awareness gives us great power to live a more fulfilled and happy life.

Cayce says the following, "For he, or she, that is without fear is free indeed." (5439-1) He also says, "Fear is the root of most of the ills of mankind whether of self, or what others think of self, or how self will appear to others. To overcome fear is to fill the mental, spiritual being with that which wholly casts out fear; the Love manifest in the world through Him." (5459-3)

Trusting God means knowing that He will carry you through any painful experience. He will be there for you through thick and thin, in the best of times and in the most challenging of times as well. The Light of God will fill your heart with courage. Trusting God will bring about a calmness of mind that will allow for healing to occur. We can begin to think more like God in creative ways to help solve problems, assuring the right outcome. His inspiration will direct our words and actions, inspiring us to say and do the right thing at the right time.

Trusting God insures that He will be active in our daily life with His Love, Wisdom, and Power. Know that with God all things are possible. His Light will enrich our lives in ways we cannot yet even imagine. We will be truly living and not merely existing.

God's In Charge

Kabbalah says that there are no coincidences, no chance encounters, and no random surprises. Everything is inter-connected, all part of the Oneness of the Creator.

Everything that happens, happens for a reason. Many times we are unaware of the reason for certain events in our life, but the Light of the Creator knows all.

If we were to trust more in this truth, with absolute certainty that God is in charge, our lives will not only be more peaceful, but our problems will work out much smoother and quicker. *There is a master plan behind all chaos.* Despite appearances the universe is always conspiring for our good.

The ego, in its attempt to keep us off balance, tries to conceal the cause of the chaos. Our job is to know the truth and to look past the ego's attempts. Kabbalah teaches us that the Light is constantly present. This truth will always set us free from emotional discomfort and negative thoughts. The greatest barrier to true self-development lies in our tendency to belittle ourselves, to feel that we are inadequate to meet the challenge. If we are relying solely on our own power, fear is justified. But when we practice applying absolute certainty knowing all things are possible with God, success comes in many different ways.

The Cayce readings tell us, "It is not only our privilege, but our duty to have faith in ourselves. We are workers together with God, and when we doubt ourselves, we doubt the God within." (262-18)

Kabbalah teaches that certainty does not mean we always get what we want. But we always get what we need for our spiritual growth, because the Light is hidden within the obstacles of life.

When any obstacle appears, remember we have created it by planting some negative seed in past thoughts or actions.

Realizing our obstacles as opportunities, we become true creators in our lives. Some of the ways to build certainty on a daily basis in order to have a reservoir in times of challenge are:

1) Meditation
2) Prayer
3) Gratitude for the problem and the lesson to be learned.
4) Being in service to others.
5) Sharing

Keeping The Faith

The main ingredient in trusting is faith. Faith is an inner knowing that allows our trust to manifest. When faith lives within us, we have true freedom.

Cayce says, "Faith is an attribute of the soul. It is the inner spiritual knowledge of the Creative Forces of the universe." (262-18) Also, "Faith is victory for where there is faith rightly placed there is no failure, but true success." (262-18)

Whenever we are trusting our intuition, our sixth sense, we are working with an alternate thought system that connects us to the Endless World. The more we use it, the more we strengthen it.

Cayce confirms this with the following, "Faith is developed by the use of it. It cannot be taught or forced, neither—if true—can it be destroyed. In the exercising of faith, there comes to each that which may be given to another for his enlightenment."(262-18)

Trust is very important because it allows us to move forward without hesitancy. This hastens the manifestation process here on earth. God desires us to trust more and more, so we can see the positive movement in our lives that trust affords. *Kabbalah says our rewards are in proportion to the faith and trust we have in the Light.*

We can see trust in action every time we are driving on a two-lane highway with traffic coming

towards us. We trust that the oncoming cars will stay
in their lane. We can extend that same kind of trust to
God, knowing that He will take care and provide for
us each and every day.

When we really get strong enough to turn
every aspect of our lives over to Him, and inject
absolute certainty, miracles start to happen
effortlessly. Because God sees the big picture, we
can truly trust Him with everything.

The power of trust is as enormous as our
willingness to let go. When we start working on trust
power, fulfillment happens, peace happens, Light
happens!

Cayce speaks of the Patriarch Abraham
regarding faith and trust. "...Abraham, the son of
faith, the author of faith offered - or was willing to
offer - his only son, his physical heir; knowing that
there must be a purpose from that Inner Voice as to
that command." (2174-2)

He also had more to say on faith. "Faith is a
bridge that spans the gulf from the seen to the unseen.
It is often all we have left when everything seems
against us. With this in mind, how diligently should
we cultivate and seek to increase our faith when all is
going well with us, in order that it may be a strong
fortress when the storms of life begin to beat upon
us." (262-18)

Cayce goes on to say, "In times of trial, let us think of the faith that has sustained others in trouble far greater than ours." (262-18)

Divine surrender to the Light is our way to achieve personal success.

By accepting *what is*, and asking, "What is the lesson here?" keeps the channel open to the Light. By asking for God's will to be made manifest, will attune us to His plan.

Trusting allows us to surrender to the divine. When we push past the ego's fears and doubts and apply certainty to all situations, the Light comes.

Just by saying, *Let thy will be done*, activates the Light. Try it. You'll be amazed.

We can then become earthly vessels for the Will of heaven.

When you completely turn your life over to God and become proactive, you ask for His guidance, and it is He who does the work through you.

Some days, there is a busy current of work energy that moves you along, and some days are more passive.

Give it time.

We are so accustomed to keeping busy and "doing" every day, that sometimes we forget it is okay to just do nothing and rest in His Love.

His timing is always perfect.

We each have a Higher Self (Divine Voice) that actually has the plan for the day already mapped

75

out for us. All we need to do is ask the Light and listen to the Voice which is in contact with the Light of the Creator.

Soon you start to realize that when you make this attunement, your Higher Self will show you the activity of the day.

When your trusting mechanism is really on, you then allow your Higher Self to do it, through you, whatever it is which needs to be done.

Our biggest challenge in doing this is our ego, our lower self. The ego, out of fear, wants to control everything all of the time and does not easily let go. This is where our knowledge and will come in. We need to surrender the logic.

The more we practice letting go and letting God, the better and quicker the results will be in our lives. Pretty soon, seeing the better results, we know we are finally moving in the current with God at the helm. We don't have to try to control anything. Now we can have more fun and enjoy greater freedom.

A major teaching of Kabbalah is that the goal of life is to merge with God.

When we realize this truth, we don't have to do anything. We don't have to go anywhere. We need only to attune with the eternal constant Presence of the Divine, the Light of the Creator, right here, right now.

The Caboose

Here is a little analogy to help keep us on track. As you probably know, the last car of a freight train is the caboose. This car is mainly for the use of the train crew and railroad workmen.

Also, the front of the train is called the locomotive. I like to think of God as the locomotive in life and myself as the caboose, sort of going along for the ride. Not that there is no action to take, just that God leads. Where He leads, I will follow. After all, I am a part of the train.

It is much easier getting to my everyday destination being the caboose. I used to try to be the locomotive, but after many derailments, I resigned myself to not doing that anymore. Besides, the caboose gets there along with the locomotive every time. I trust the locomotive. I know that it knows where it's going, always keeping me on the right track.

Being the caboose was real humbling at first. I had a judgment about being last. To me, the caboose was not the most prestigious position to be. Up front, that was where it was at, so I thought.

I like being the caboose now. Less stress, more fun, and I really get to relax. My mind is without a doubt enjoying the ride so much better. I laugh more. I feel better, too. What a wonderful difference it has made in my life. I am now actually happy to be the caboose. If anyone were to ask me if I would like to be the locomotive, I would say, "No thank you, I prefer being the caboose." Some people may laugh but I really don't care. When I look inside the caboose I see the truth, and to me, that is all that matters.

PART TWO

PROACTIVE

vs.

REACTIVE

Chapter 6

CHOOSING NOT TO REACT

Kabbalah says we always have a choice to either react to a negative situation which shuts down the Light from coming through, or we can detach from our five senses, use our sixth sense, and then express our proactive nature (caring, sharing, doing a good deed, understanding) to become more like the Creator.

The use of our sixth sense, this inner knowing which Kabbalah speaks about, allows us to more easily use resistance to any possible negative emotional reactions. *This spiritual knowledge, when activated and applied daily on the playing field of life, transforms our human nature and gives us greater peace.*

Even if we momentarily feel anger towards someone, we can quickly diffuse any negative emotions by applying our spiritual awareness.

When we can remember that our negative feelings are our real challenge, we can turn the table around by asking the Light for assistance, using resistance and being proactive.

If you find it difficult to change your reactive nature at a certain moment, and you then change it, know that the change is real and you have received more Light.

As Light-beings, it is important to be aware that the force known as intuition is included in the Light as well. This is our spiritual sixth sense, the one above and beyond our ego or body's five senses.

It is that still small Voice that relates the Truth. It is that nudge, that hunch, that gut feeling, that inner prompting we all experience at times. The body's five senses can easily deceive us and the opponent uses them often to do so.

Be on guard. The Light will never deceive us. Truth will always set us free from the opponent's lies. That is why connecting with the Light is so important to our freedom and happiness.

To repeat, *it is important to remember to ask to be a channel for the Light.* The opponent is seemingly quite strong at times and all of us need help. It is there in the 99 percent realm waiting to respond to our call.

Remember to remember spirit is another magic key. We can lift those ten curtains or veils that are holding back the Light. By resisting

82

pessimism and negative thinking, more of the Light we seek can enter into our minds.

There are many situations in everyday life that confront and challenge us, causing us to react. When they appear, sometimes we are not aware about not reacting, but instead, we instantly react.

This unawareness causes the pain and guilt within. With awareness, we can choose not to react, and go through situations more peacefully, bringing in more Light. We can stop ourselves from feeling hurt, guilty, or any other negative emotion.

By becoming aware that this situation is a gift in disguise, knowing that *it is only a test,* can help us stay centered as well.

In Kabbalah we learn that the reason we react to negative traits in others is *because we have those same traits in our ego selves, but not necessarily to the same degree.* The Cayce readings also advise: "Faults in others are reflected first in self." (452-3) The world is our mirror. If you want to know how well you are doing, look at your relationships. What are they reflecting back to you? Love or fear?

As mentioned earlier, whenever we are challenged in any way, to stop and remember: *The problem is not the problem. Our reaction to the problem is our real enemy.*

This is the human part of our mind that instantly feels threatened by negative stimuli. At this strong emotional level, we are operating with only our five senses.

Will You React or Proact?

If you look to be helpful to others, but find they are lacking in appreciation, don't get upset and react by mumbling that you're never going to help anyone again. Just smile and know that the Light appreciates all that you do. The situation is always about you and the Light. Rewards often come from other sources than those we assist. Just keep on choosing to be a channel for the Light.

If you are at work and someone starts to harshly judge your capabilities, there is no need to react. Know at that moment, if you start to feel upset, you can stop, take a breath, and try to love more, understanding it is an opportunity to forgive.

When you are at home and a family member points out something you didn't do, that you said you were going to do, if you begin to react, you can stop, choose again, and be proactive, like apologize. Even if insincere at first, it is still being proactive and it will help the situation. Your emotions will be lifted.

If you receive a phone call from someone who is having a bad day and that person starts to attack you, it's your choice whether to react or not.

Shutting down our reactive mechanism is something very worthwhile to master. It will transform our lower nature, bring in more Light and help to create miracles. We will get stronger.

Cayce gave us more wonderful wisdom in the following reading when he said, "Try to see self in the other's place. And this will bring the basic spiritual forces that must be the prompting influence in the experience of each soul, if it would grow in grace, in knowledge, in understanding; not only of its relationship to God, its relationship to its fellow man, but its relationship in the home and in the social life." (2936-2)

Life's events sometimes move quickly and take us off guard. It is very helpful to be vigilant if your negative emotions start to well up.

It is like hitting a pitch from a fast ball pitcher. You need to stand ready and be aware of its speed. The more you remember to focus, the quicker you will learn to proact instead of react.

Our solar plexus gives us the clue. It is the seat of our emotions that needs to be watched. If it starts to bubble with anxiety or any other negative emotion, we need to interrupt our tendency to react automatically. A self-centered person is a reactive person. With practice, we can transform our lower negative reactive nature each and every time.

Cayce reinforced this with the following, "...the conquering of self is truly greater then were one to conquer many worlds..." (115-1)

85

Peace is our goal and it can be accomplished when we learn to master our emotions. Life does present us with many opportunities to transform ourselves into more God-like beings.

Kabbalah says: It is a process that will change our lives and bring us greater freedom, fulfillment and happiness within.

Unconditional love means we need to love in spite of what is being done to us. People are messengers of the Light and it is important to trust in the Light.

The universe is always talking to us.

We must try to see the Light in everything and in everyone, looking beyond any of their negative ego traits we happen to notice. *That is not their true self.* We are all on the same journey to the same place. The more we can recognize this, the more we can truly help each other.

The following experiences could indicate that you are starting to live in God's Kingdom of Light:

* When you are seeing the oneness in all people, and act with this knowing.

* When the Peace of God is surrounding you more times than not.

* When the Love of God is fully in your heart and you realize that love is all there is.

* When the Light of God is illuminating your mind and you graciously start helping others.

* When worry thoughts begin to disappear.

* When you are feeling joy.

* When you find you're smiling more throughout the day.

* When something that used to bother you a whole lot no longer does.

* When you are relying more on God's power than on your own and you're seeing better results.

* When it is easy to forgive.

Suppression

Kabbalah advises that emotional resistance and behavioral restriction, without being immediately followed by proactivity, breeds suppression. This knowledge eliminates suppression, which is of the ego, that shuts off areas of the mind it does not want to deal with. Suppression is a temporary fix that will not maintain itself and will eventually explode from the pressure.

Cayce confirms this by saying, "For to hold grudges, to hold malice, to hold those things that create or bring contention, only builds the barrier to prevent thy own inner self enjoying peace and content." (1608-1)

Resistance is a definitive key to bringing in lasting Light. We may have to struggle a little at first in applying resistance, but soon calmness and peace come with the Light. The more we practice resistance, the easier it becomes to apply and the quicker we start to feel better in every pressured situation.

Some Points to Remember:

1. When you react, it causes chaos. Chaos brings more challenges.
2. Resist. Stop. Take a breath. Be certain that the Light WILL work out the situation for the better.
3. Ask to be a channel for the Light.
4. Listen for inner guidance.
5. Proact

Our spiritual will power is very strong. We need to learn how to truly activate it to full capacity. Knowledge of the truth can help us to increase our will power. By knowing we receive positive results in using resistance helps us to increase our will power.

We can heal our minds through the application of spiritual will power and start to see immediate results in the effects of the Light that is being generated in and around us.

A Perfect Universe

No matter what the outer picture of our life looks like, this is a perfect universe to learn our lessons and grow to become more like God.

When we bring in more Light, negativity and darkness vanish. Our consciousness expands each time we are effective in applying needed resistance. We can access greater freedom from negative thoughts by using resistance and not reacting. It is our Light in action creating more Light.

Seeing positive results will give us more of a conviction to keep applying resistance to challenges.

Kabbalah asks you to test out this ancient formula and see how it works in your life.

I have personally tested it and it has become an important part of my everyday life. We are always growing and being tested.

Several years ago, due to financial challenges, my wife and I had to move from a large three bedroom house we were renting, to a small two bedroom apartment.

Our apartment was on the second floor and the ceiling at the bottom of the stairwell at the entrance was low. The night before our baby grand piano (nicknamed Orca) was to be delivered from storage, Karen and I rearranged the furniture. She told me, "For some reason, I just can't picture the baby grand here. It belongs in a bigger place where a large audience can enjoy your music."

The next day when the moving company pulled up out front, the name on the truck was BOS. A sure sign that something was up. God is the Boss. When they rolled open the van doors, Orca was the only item on board. The movers tried to bring the piano up the stairs, but it could not get past the first three steps. The ceiling was too low.

I was told that the piano wasn't going to make it up the stairs. "There must be a way," I said, in shock. They politely tried again, but it was obvious this was not going to happen.

With a homeless piano and the clock ticking away on the moving van, I tried to still my mind, invoking the Light. Inspiration came.

The Association for Research and Enlightenment was located a half a block away. I quickly ran over there to ask if Orca could be placed in the auditorium on loan. The administrator agreed to take her in.

It was a win-win. They had permission to use the piano for conferences, and I was able to play whenever the room was available.

That night I ended up playing for The Forum (an A.R.E. conference) in the auditorium. Not only that, but soon I started volunteering to play for many of their other conferences, and even recorded my two piano solo CDs there as well. The spiritual energy vortex at the A.R.E. is amazing.

Cayce says, "For until ye are willing to lose thyself in service, ye may not indeed know that which He has promised to give— to all." (1599-1)

Kabbalists tell us the key to overcoming self is *detaching from our five senses and being more proactive.* In times of stress, we again need to stop, take a breath and love more.

The earth is of a negative polarity and so is reactivity. By applying resistance, we also overcome the influences of the negative magnetics of the planet. This causes us to change our human nature into a more positive God-like nature, the goal of our journey while here on the planet.

When we change, the world changes.

By doing the spiritual work, we get the positive results. This can be proven time and time again as the secrets of Kabbalah and Cayce's wisdom are applied in our everyday lives.

We no longer have to be robots reacting to negative external stimuli. By the use of resistance, we can change our inner nature and our outer circumstances. We don't have to feel angry or jealous. And we no longer need to yell or brood over anything or anyone.

Kabbalah teaches that challenges will connect us to more Light of the Creator. We can use this secret as great leverage for overcoming our reactive behavior.

This can be done by re-programming our minds and accepting the truth that nothing really is bad—it just is.

Because life is a schoolhouse, lessons need to be learned. Although a situation may appear to be bad at the time, it is only our negative emotions needing to be overcome that we are reacting to.

Emotions are like waves upon the water. They come and they go. We need not be ruled by our negative emotions.

Seeing the truth in every situation will help to set us free from our emotional conflicts. Kabbalah and Cayce teach us how to see and know the truth.

Through obstacles come opportunities for more Light and growth, something the ego does not want to hear.

Cayce said the following when asked the question, what is truth? "That which makes aware of the Divine within each and every activity: that is of the mental, the material, the spiritual self—and is a growth in each and every soul...What is Truth? That which makes aware to the inmost self or the soul the divine and its purposes with that soul." (262-81)

When we restrict our behavior from "acting out" our negative feelings about a person or a situation, and then behave proactively, the Light comes. This is our God-self in action.

Beware of Complacency

Another area of reactive behavior that our ego likes to play hide and seek in, is complacency, which means self-satisfaction accompanied by unawareness of actual dangers. Even when things are going well in certain areas of our lives, sometimes our human behavior needs correction in that area.

However, the ego stays put and we do nothing to change. The Light, always seeking to help us grow beyond our ego's stronghold, will send us a challenge to awaken us to our complacency.

This will help us to change our nature. It will force us to be more proactive. This cleansing is always ongoing because of all the stuff we have to clear in becoming balanced and more like God.

Challenges Equal Opportunities

When challenges come, it is important to remember there is never anyone to blame.

93

It is simply the Light of the Creator sending us an opportunity for more Light to come to us.

When we choose to transform our human nature and be proactive, the Light does come and the challenge is overcome. Kabbalah says that eventually everything works out for the best, all of the time.

As mentioned earlier, *the bigger the challenge in our lives, to the same degree does more Light come.* Knowing this can help us in our time of overcoming self. Again, just realizing the truth will give us a powerful boost of positive energy we can use in our favor.

The Light of the Creator knows how strong we are. It also knows how much we can handle at any given period in our lives and will never overload our capacity to overcome.

If we keep on remembering that God lives inside of us, we can call upon the Light at any time for help. The Light will only come in when invited. Everything can be overcome with the Light. Turn it on and you will see.

If for any reason we don't listen to that inner prompting when challenges come, you'll know it because the challenges will increase.

Therefore, it is best to get on with it as quickly as possible when any challenge appears. This can save us from extra pressure in the future. We must not become spiritual procrastinators.

In a reading when Cayce was asked, "How may I best overcome procrastination?" his answer was, "By applying self in the ways in which Today, if ye will hear His voice, harden not your hearts." (5018-1)

At other subtle levels of ego interference that keep us from enjoying more Light from the Creator, *Kabbalah says that even the act of telling a fib needs to be curbed.* We need to stop our robotic responses and negative behavior.

The more positivity we can inject into any situation, the more positivity the cosmic universe will send back.

And the reverse is also true. What we put in, is what we get in return. Our goal is to become better than we currently are. No matter how good a person is, there is always room for improvement.

Cayce had this to say about choice: "Each individual has the choice, which no one has the **Right** to supercede—even God does not!" (254-102)

"Know that the birthright of every soul is choice, or will." (2329-1) "As from the beginning, choice is that which separated the entity from the Creative Forces or makes for its being one with same." (877-1)

Always choose to be a channel for the Light, no matter what!

Again, proactively resisting our reactive behavior connects us to the 99 percent reality.

Reacting negatively to any situation leaves us in the one percent darkness. We do have a choice.

As mentioned before, it does take discipline, inner strength and calling in the Light for assistance to help us overcome our challenges, but the more we do it, the easier it gets.

Cayce spoke about resistance and proactivity in this reading. "Never so act, in any manner, in any inclination, that there may ever be an experience of regret within self. Let the moves and the discourteousness, the unkindness, all come from the other. Better to be abased and have the peace within!...act ever in the way ye would like to be acted toward. No matter what others say or even do, do as ye would be done by; and then the peace that has been promised is indeed thine own." (1183-3) The following lyrics on the next page exemplify the gift of choice.

"IT'S UP TO YOU (What Will You Choose?)"

Whatcha gonna do if the well runs dry
Will you sit right down and then start to cry
Or will you look straight up to the shining sky
It's Up To You - What Will You Choose?

You can choose again if you need some time
You can go inside and then change your mind
Wish upon a star if you're so inclined
It's Up To You - What Will You Choose?

You can choose to be happy
You can choose to be sad
Making up your mind
Is the greatest gift that we all have

You can choose again if you want some fun
If you're choosing love fear is on the run
There's no better choice when the day's begun
It's Up To You - What Will You Choose?

Words and Music by Elliot Chiprut

Chapter 7

PREVIOUS LIVES

Both the Zohar and the Edgar Cayce material, along with several other spiritual world traditions, teach that our soul returns to earth from the 99 percent non-physical world with gifts, talents, strengths and weaknesses from our previous lives.

As mentioned, earth is a schoolroom ordained by Divine Law, where certain lessons in ego control need to be experienced. Individuals must return to the Earth over and over again, until they have found the mastery of energy (life), which is their reason for taking physical embodiment in the first place. When we desire, we take on a physical body here in the physical world to accomplish this. This is called reincarnation.

We do this to help further our growth by learning to be more proactive in areas of our lives that need correction, or balancing, from past life experiences. Kabbalah calls the correction process, "Tikun."

Everyone in a physical body has some kind of Tikun they are working on. Whatever we find uncomfortable for us to deal with is part of our Tikun. The people that upset us are also part of our Tikun.

Kabbalah says there are many areas in our life in which we can have a Tikun. These include: health, family relationships, intimate relationships, friendships, money, and work.

Another way to detect our Tikun is if we find ourselves in a situation where we get easily embarrassed.

Encountering My Tikun

Many years ago my ego got busted in a most embarrassing way. After having much success in my music career, I was now married with two young sons. My finances began to wane and I needed to create more income. Fortunately, my father was a manufacturer of ladies sportswear in Manhattan and gave me a job in production. I learned the garment business quickly and had to put aside my musical aspirations for a time.

One day, a large order of suits for a big retail chain account needed to be delivered at a certain hour. If not delivered on time, this order would be cancelled. We did have two workers in the shipping department, but on that day one of them didn't show up. Soon, I found myself at the back end of two double racks of suits, pushing them up 7th Avenue and across town to the retailer's west side warehouse.

My ego took a big hit in humility, as I kept worrying that someone I knew might see me, the famous songwriter/record producer, pushing these racks uptown. I returned unblemished, except for a bruised ego. I got over it and freed myself in that area.

Tikun is similar to Karma, past life cause and effect, which Cayce spoke often about. Although he said Karma may also be good sometimes, bringing blessings in return.

This is not to say that all of our needed corrections come from past lives. Some repeat over and over in our current lifetime.

Cayce agrees with this. "Cause and effect to many are the same as Karma. Karma is that brought over, while cause and effect may exist in the one material experience only." (2981-2) "Karma is then, that that has been in the past builded as indifference to that known to be right. Taking chances, as it were—"Will do better tomorrow—this suits my purpose today—I'll do better tomorrow." (257-78) "What is Karma but giving way to impulse?" (622-6)

We come to earth to transform our negativity and to earn the beneficence of the Creator. We can do this by being more proactive in areas of our lives where we need to get stronger. Kabbalah also says we will encounter every scenario to personally achieve the correction we came to earth to achieve. The truth sets us free. I have found it comforting to know that we are always exactly where we need to be for the purpose of achieving our spiritual correction. *All is in Divine Order.*

Cayce says, "Know that in whatever state ye find thyself, that-at the moment-is best for thee. (369-16)

Tikun Removal Tips

The awareness of a Tikun is designed to help keep us out of the victim role we sometimes fall into. Trying to avoid our Tikun will only bring us more chaos. Dealing proactively with it will bring in more Light and fulfillment, which is its purpose.

The application of resistance to reactivity will help us deal with those difficult circumstances that are part of our Tikun. Kabbalah says that every time a person is reactive, it sets off a negative occurrence either in this lifetime or in a future lifetime. If the behavior correction is not made, it will continue to carry over into a future life until it is met and overcome.

We may also need to apply resistance in order to remove our Tikun and be more proactive in the following areas as well:

1. **Judgment** - Sometimes we get caught up in our reaction to other people's behavior, or perhaps by only hearing one side of a story. Judge not unless you want to be judged.

2. **Laziness** - When inspiration strikes and we need to do something, but procrastinate instead, we must resist laziness and move forward. Remember we do have a strong will.

3. **Ego Chatter** - Whenever you find yourself in a group of people who are bragging about their possessions, social status, etc., try to keep your mouth closed if you feel an impulse to join in. This is your ego.

4. **Expectations** - When things in life seem to be materializing for you and then suddenly go out to sea, know that, once again, all is in divine order. There will be something much better coming. Resist disappointment, you will understand later on.

5. **Evil Impulses** - Sometimes when you meet someone who starts gossiping about another person, refrain from joining in. Instead, silently witness the Light in the situation. Resist this negative temptation and you will add more Light. Try changing the conversation.

6. **Guilt** - Even if we mess up and do something wrong, there is no need to take a guilt trip. This

wrongdoing is only an indication that we lost control of ourselves in that situation which needs to be corrected in the future. There will be another opportunity. Forgiveness works wonders.

7. **Shyness** - Being shy with someone or with something can hold us back. Recognition of this can help us to overcome. Call on the Light.

8. **Saying No** - Finding it hard to say "no" to people when appropriate is important. The Light will give you the strength.

9. **Confronting** - Having difficulty confronting someone when we must can also be overcome by calling on the Light. You'd be amazed. Try to remember the truth will set everyone free.

Edgar Cayce and Reincarnation

Edgar Cayce gave 2,500 past life readings from the source, or spiritual realm, to people from all walks of life. Numerous letters and documents bear witness to the accuracy of so many of them.

When giving a reading, he sometimes used the term "the entity" referring to the immortal individual, the soul, who incarnates over and over again gaining the needed lessons to perfect itself. He also mentioned that our problems, our strengths and weaknesses, are mirrored in our acquaintances and experiences.

Both Cayce and the Kabbalah say that we pick our family, sex, location, time, and economic level with each new incarnation, all designed for the perfect growth of each soul.

Cayce gave this life reading for an eleven month old boy telling the parents their child had been a famous composer in a previous life. He said, "In the musical abilities should the entity be trained from the beginning. There is the natural intent and interest towards things of the artistic nature and temperament. There are the abilities to use the voice, as well as the abilities in playing most ANY instrument- if the opportunity is given; especially in the composition, in the natures of composition as well as the playing itself. Symphonies, all forms of musical interludes and the like, should be the trainings to which the entity would be subjected- that it may be given the greater opportunities. And, as soon as he is capable of such, insist upon beginning with the piano, as a playing, as a means of entertaining. And the natural ear for harmony will soon be indicated in the activities of the entity...

Before this the entity was in the Austrian or Hungarian land. There the entity was an unusual individual, in the name of Liszt; being a composer as well as a musician. And as its activities through the experience were such as to make for certain characters of music, these in part will be of special interest to the entity in the present. The comparison may be easily seen, to be sure, as to the faults, the failures, as well as the activities in which the entity then throughout the experience rose to its place or position in the musical world. That is why, then, the nickname Franz is suggested; for the entity was Franz Liszt." (2584-1)

It is not so important to know who or what we were in a prior lifetime, e.g., a king, queen, or some famous person, rather than how previous lifetimes may have created certain circumstances or scenarios which we need to learn lessons from in this lifetime.

It is helpful to know and understand that current difficult situations may have had its origin from the past. We can then be more proactive, sensitive, and tolerant of others and ourselves.

It is also good to remember that all things happen for a reason and work together for good, except in the ego's judgment. Each time we are proactive, life can become more of an exciting creative adventure.

Cayce was questioned during a reading, "What will convince me of reincarnation?" His answer was, "An experience." (956-1)

I can relate to this reading from Cayce. When I was six-years-old, my sister received a piano for her eleventh birthday. In a short time, I was sitting by her side watching and listening to her play songs that she'd heard on the radio, all by ear.

Before long, I started playing those popular songs on the piano by ear, too. Like my sister, all I had to do was hear the music and somehow I just "knew" how to play it. It came naturally to both of us.

At the age of eight, my mom brought me to the Manhattan School of Music for my first piano lesson. The teacher played a simple melody from the sheet music in order for me to learn how to read the musical notes. I had committed the melody to memory and didn't practice reading it at home.

When I returned the following week, while playing the lesson, a gust of wind through the open window blew the sheet music onto the floor. But I kept on playing without missing a note. To my surprise, the teacher expelled me from class. I was not teachable since I played by ear.

I believe my musical talent is a carryover from a previous life, or lives, when I had learned music. Without being able to read a note, I have written over a thousand songs in several genres ranging from pop music to waltzes.

Both Kabbalah and Cayce agree that we each come to earth with a specific spiritual mission to receive fulfillment and remove chaos through self correction. If we do not complete our spiritual correction in one lifetime, the soul returns in another

107

lifetime, a different body, to continue the correction process. The correction process can only take place in a physical body, where the chaos occurred to begin with.

In reading 262-40, the question, "From what may *anyone* be saved?" was asked of the sleeping Cayce, who replied: "Only from themselves! That is, their individual hell; they dig it with their own desires!"

The Cayce readings frequently advised the proper attitude regarding reincarnation and karma. "If the experiences are ever used for self-indulgence, self-aggrandizement, self-exaltation, each entity does so to its OWN undoing, or creates for self that as has been termed or called karma - and must be met. And in meeting every error, in meeting every trial, in meeting every temptation - whether these be mental or really physical experiences - the manner and purpose and approach to same should be ever in that attitude, 'Not my will but Thine, O God, be done in and through me.'" (1224-1)

Cayce was asked this question, "If a soul fails to improve itself, what becomes of it?"

He answered, "That's why the reincarnation, why it reincarnates, that it may have the opportunity. Can the will of man continue to defy its Maker?" (826-8)

According to Cayce, another main purpose of reincarnation is to allow individuals to become aware of their true spiritual nature and their ultimate relationship with one another. The choices we make determine the next set of potential experiences we encounter. We constantly meet the consequences of previous deeds and attitudes.

Here are some examples found in the Cayce readings that shed more light:

In reading (3125-2), Cayce said, "In another experience we find that the entity was a chemist, and she used many of those various things for the producing of itching in others. She finds it (allergies) in herself in the present!"

And in another reading Cayce explains, "The basic reaction of these (deafness) are somewhat of the karmic nature...Then, do not close the ears, the mind or the heart again to those who plead for aid." (3526-1)

In a life reading for a thirty-nine-year old Jewish rabbi, he learned that his previous incarnation was in early America as a French Catholic trader. Before that he was among the children of Israel in the Old Testament times, and before that a Zoroastrian in Persia. He asked if he should remain a rabbi or go into business and was told: "...yes, as a rabbi in its TRUEST sense; that is - a teacher, a minister. NOT as bound by creeds! Not as bound by modes! Not as bound by any law!

COORDINATE the teachings, the philosophies of the east and the west, the oriental and the occidental, the new truths and the old...Correlate not the differences, but where all religions meet— THERE IS ONE GOD! 'Know, O Israel, the Lord thy God is ONE!'

...Hast thou not found that the ESSENCE, the truth, the REAL truth is ONE? Mercy and justice; peace and harmony. For without Moses and his leader, Joshua, (that was bodily Jesus) there IS no Christ. CHRIST is not a man! Jesus was the man; Christ the messenger; Christ in all ages, Jesus in one, Joshua in another, Melchizedek in another; THESE be those that led Judaism! These be they that came as that child of promise, as to the children of promise; and the promise is in thee that ye lead as He has given thee, 'Feed my sheep.'" (991-1)

Astrology

The Zohar tells us that we are born into this world under a specific celestial influence. This is determined by deeds in our past lives. Through prayer, meditation, and good deeds, we can overcome negative influences.

When Cayce was asked, "Would it be well for me to make a study of astrology?"

The answer was, "Well for everyone to make a study of astrology!" (311-10)

However, Cayce clarified the relationship of astrology and free will, "...but let it be understood here, no action of any planet or the phases of the sun, the moon or any of the heavenly bodies surpass the rule of man's will power, the power given by the Creator of man in the beginning, when he became a living soul, with the power of choosing for himself." (3744-3)

Many years ago an acquaintance of mine who was the vice president of Mercury Records invited me to lunch. "Do you believe in astrology?" he asked.

At that time, I was only aware of the astrology columns in the newspapers. To me, it seemed like superficial entertainment. He asked if I wanted to invest $50 in myself. There was an excellent intuitive astrologer overseas who could help with insights into life. He highly recommended him. Looking for more direction in my life at the time, I sent an American Express check to the hills of Italy.

In less than two weeks, I received a ten-page astrology report. It was quite surprising to read all of the accurate personal information, which included talents, past lives, possibilities of the future, and things I needed to work on in this life. All from a person thousands of miles away who didn't even know me! Especially since I had only sent him my name, date, time and place of birth. I did not even mention who had recommended him. He made me a believer right away, confirming that I was a writer who could make much money through music and should be in the field of entertainment. As he put it, "Of this there is no doubt at all."

In addition to personal information, he gave me a list of metaphysical books to read including some Edgar Cayce material. He said I would understand them because of my past lives. I had apparently known much of this information before and needed to refresh my memory.

As I look back, I can now see the astrologer was connecting to the 99 percent realm where all of this information is available. I didn't know it at the time.

The information from my astrology chart caused a great shift in me, as I started to connect with my real inner Self. I was never a reader in school, or at home, but the information from these recommended metaphysical books had me glued to the pages. I couldn't get enough. My soul was so thirsty, I would read book after book for days and days.

Whenever I had the time, I would read about all the different religions, Edgar Cayce, the Old and New Testaments, Ascended Master Teaching, and many other esoteric books that filled my soul. I was connecting with the Light and this made me very happy. Later on, I also became a long time student of *A Course in Miracles.* The study of Kabbalah has now increased my spiritual awareness as well, bringing more Light from the Creator for me to share. In all of my searching, I've found there is one truth: GOD IS LOVE.

Our purpose, once again, for all of this self-correction work here on earth and for reincarnation is to allow us to become more God-like by filling ourselves with Light from the Creator. In each lifetime, we are becoming a better person.

When we reach a certain Light quotient in our total being, we no longer have to reincarnate into a physical body. We graduate to the Upper World and to a higher level of existence and conscious awareness. We become masters and are no longer subject to the physical laws of life and death here on earth. We then actualize our eternal being, as in the beginning when the morning stars sang.

Chapter 8

SPIRITUAL TOOL BOX

In life there are many physical tools like a hammer and screwdriver that make working in the material world a whole lot easier. There are also spiritual tools, which this chapter is all about. They can help us in our spiritual work of overcoming self, or ego.

Because Kabbalah is the blueprint of the universe, it provides man with the tools and methods for connecting to spiritual Light. It is our own actions or lack of actions that determine whether we live in darkness or Light. Due to the seeming power of our ego, or opponent, it is important to receive as much help as possible. Victory will bring great freedom, happiness, and fulfillment.

As mentioned before, the purpose of our lives is *to transform our human nature into a more God-like nature.* It is wonderful to learn new concepts, but the litmus test is *how well we can apply what we know in our daily living.* Cayce confirms this: "It is not how much one knows that counts, but how well one applies that (which) it knows." (270-33)

Spiritual tools, when diligently used, can help make our task easier. Here is a tool box of options to choose from. I invite you to use what you feel will be right for you.

1. Meditation

Kabbalah says the purpose of meditation is not to just feel comfortable and relaxed, but to help us make the connection to the 99% realm, the Endless World, and to bring in that Light to assist us in improving our everyday lives.

The Hebrew word for meditation is *kavanah* which means "direction." The Zohar says that everything in this world depends upon the world above, and whatever is agreed upon above is also accepted below.

The Cayce readings had more information on meditation. "Meditation is the listening to the Divine within." (1861-19)

"It is not musing, not daydreaming; but as ye find your bodies made up of the physical, mental and spiritual, it is attuning of the mental body and the physical body to its spiritual source." (281-41)

"If ye will MEDITATE, open thy heart, thy mind! Let thy body and mind be channels that YE may DO the things ye ask God to do for you! Thus you come to know Him." (281-41)

In several of his readings, Cayce suggested facing east as the best position for meditation.

Another method recommended in the readings was to connect with nature.

"Meditate oft. Separate thyself for a season from the cares of the world. Get close to nature and learn from the lowliest of that which manifests in nature, in the earth, in the birds, in the trees, in the grass, in the flowers, in the bees; that the life of each is a manifesting, is a song of glory to its Maker. And do thou likewise!" (1089-3)

We all want to receive the truth, the Light, and direction to help set us free from ourselves. By stilling our minds of worldly thoughts through resistance, increasing spiritual desire controlled by will, and closing down our five senses, we can open up a channel to the Light. This can give us access to direction from our Creator who is above and within us. A peaceful mind is a treasure beyond measure. Once this is fully achieved, there really is nothing else. It is the supreme goal for living a happy, loving, joyous, and fulfilled life.

Kabbalah and Cayce both recommend meditation. It can also help us to be more proactive by giving us additional inner strength.

117

How To Meditate

A candle to represent the Light of the Creator is recommended. It is interesting to note that when a candle is used to light another candle, its own flame is not diminished. This is symbolic of our sharing Light with others. It is never diminished. If anything, the more Light you share, the more you are giving to the world. The more you are expanding the Light of the Creator, the more is given back to you.

It is best to be in a sitting position, without crossing your arms or legs to promote the flow of energy.

Keep your hands on your lap, relaxed with palms up. Thumb and index finger may be touching.

You may also want to have your heels touching each other and your tongue touching the roof of your mouth, behind your front teeth.

Meditate at the same time and same place every day to discipline the ego mind, preferably before meals.

Breathe in a relaxed and even manner, in through the nose, and out through the mouth.

When breathing in, breathe in the Light of the Creator, as your intention.

When breathing out, let go of any stress, tension, worry, and anxiety. You can close your eyes or keep them open and focus on a candle. Gazing at a flame in a fireplace, or staring at a body of water, works well, too.

There are many proven physical benefits to meditation, including stress reduction. Your health can improve as well as your mind. When the question was asked of the sleeping Cayce, "How can I improve memory and concentration?" He answered, "Study well that which has been given through these sources on meditation. Through meditation may the greater help be gained." (987-2)

I know that by practicing meditation for over thirty-five years, I've been able to feel it's positive effects in my life. Meditation is a wonderful discipline that is more worthwhile than one can imagine. It will help bring the lower self under the influence and control of the spiritual higher self, the real you. It doesn't matter how long you meditate each day, although fifteen minutes is recommended; consistency is the key. Even if you meditate for only five minutes each morning and/or evening, you will feel the benefits of this peaceful enhancing experience.

Heart Meditation

This is a simple meditation I've used over the years. Start in the same seated position previously mentioned.

Close your eyes and keep your breathing even.

Visualize a ray of golden Light coming from the Creator into the top of your head and down into your heart, shining like a golden sun.

Stay focused on that Light in your heart.

If any outside worldly thoughts start to occur, simply dismiss them by continuing to focus on the golden Light of the sun in your heart.

This is your time to be alone with the Creator. "Be still and know that I am God." (Psalm 46:10)

With practice you will get better and better at it. You will feel the peace.

2. Prayer

Whereas meditation is listening to the Creator, prayer is talking to the Creator. Both are signals to the universe that you believe there is a higher power than yourself that can help you. It is humbleness. It is faith in action.

A helpful reminder from the Cayce readings if you should begin to be fearful about any situation: "Why worry when ye may pray? Know that the power of thyself is very limited. The power of Creative Force is unlimited." (2981-1)

Kabbalah says the Light of the Creator is always there. It never changes. The Light wants to answer all of our prayers and fulfill every desire. In order for this to happen, we need to make contact.

A calm and centered mind, as in meditation, is necessary. This is why it is important to restrict our negative behavior and watch for any unkind words, so the lines of communication do not break down due to negative energy. This will assure good contact with the Light of the Creator and the 99% Upper World. With the static removed, we can know that our messages will be received by the Light, and in turn, we will be able to receive an answer.

As in meditation, prayer at the same time and place is most helpful. It is a rewarding habit to make.

Cayce had this to say about prayer and meditation, "Then set definite periods for prayer; set definite periods for meditation. Know the difference between each. Prayer, in short, is appealing to the divine within self, the divine from without self, and meditation is keeping still in body, in mind, in heart, listening, listening, listening to the voice of thy Maker." (5368-1) "All prayer is answered. Don't tell God how to answer it." (4028-1)

Simplicity is also an important key. Be direct but simple. Kabbalah suggests that to be truly effective in our prayers, we need to have a fire burning in our hearts. The more emotion that is projected, the stronger the contact.

Cayce offered this simple prayer suggestion to a married couple. "For a period of six months, never leave the home, either of you, without offering a prayer together; 'Thy will, O God, be done in me this day.' This is not sissy; this is not weak; this is strong." (2811-3)

When convenient, lighting a candle before prayer is helpful. Prayers that are sung have more power to them. Group prayer has more power, too. People can pray together at long distances and be quite effective. All we need to do is set a time and join together. Space knows no boundary when it comes to prayers.

Cayce said, "The prayers of ten may save a city; the prayers of twenty-five may save a nation—as the prayers of **one** may! but in union there is strength." (1598-2)

Prayers for world peace are greatly needed at this time. Prayers to remove hunger from the world are needed too. Praying for more Light to come to earth can produce amazing results. All we need to do is open our hearts and send it out. God will do the rest.

The Shema Prayer

The Shema Prayer is a well-known powerful Hebrew prayer, reminding us of God and our oneness with Him. It is a declaration of faith.

This prayer is said with eyes closed at sunrise, or first light, and sunset, or before sleep. It can be recited in any language:

HEAR, O ISRAEL, THE LORD OUR GOD, THE LORD IS ONE. Hebrew Translation: SHEMA, YISRAEL, ADONAI ELOHEINO, ADONAI ECHAD .

Interestingly, this prayer is found in both the Old Testament Bible (Deuteronomy 6:4), as well as the New Testament Bible (Mark 12:29). The Name of God, made up of fourteen Hebrew letters, was derived from this Shema Prayer.

3. Gratitude

Gratitude is like a switch in your mind that when turned on brings more joy, peace, and happiness. Especially in the most challenging times, gratitude works like a healing balm resolving the stickiest situations. In the best of times, gratitude enhances our lives even further.

It is wise to channel energy into gratitude for a problem rather than spending enormous time and resources trying to figure out the answer and becoming fearful that we are inadequate.

Kabbalah says when we appreciate the Light in all things, we feel like we have it all and that gives us cosmic permission to really have it all. Through gratitude, appreciation, and thankfulness, we receive benefits and opportunities that most people only hope for.

This powerful tool can shift our consciousness to a higher level, connecting us to the Light. When worry, fear, stress and anger come knocking on our door, let gratitude answer. It chases all those negative visitors away.

Our Creator wants us to receive everything with thankfulness. This will assure blessings of enduring joy, peace and happiness.

We can overcome the opponent or ego, with sincere gratitude. This helps maintain a positive outlook.

Remember, the opponent brings us the challenge, or darkness, so we can see more Light and rise higher in consciousness to receive more joy and peace, for this we may give thanks. Both spirit and earth respond positively to the positive energy of thankfulness. It is a powerful form of proactivity, assuring us more Light.

Gratitude can be used in every situation, circumstance, and experience, both good and so-called bad. It goes beyond the rational mind and creates miracles. The more you are grateful, the happier your life becomes. It is a natural law that never fails; so simple, yet so effective.

Cayce said, "Be glad you have the opportunity to be alive at this time, and to be a part of that preparation for the coming influences of a spiritual nature that must rule the world. These are indicated, and these are part of thy experience. Be happy of it, and give thanks daily for it." (2376-3)

Gratitude can also heal resentment. Most mental ills as well as many physical ills are caused by feelings of resentment, consciously or unconsciously. It is impossible to be grateful and resentful at the same time. Whenever you are feeling any kind of resentment, you can deliberately change those feelings caused by some hurt or disappointment by thinking of something you are grateful for.

Remember disappointments are actually leading you to a better way of life by causing you to rise above your ego self. They are a blessing in disguise.

It is because of our dark experiences that we are moved to cultivate a grateful, praiseful, and thankful state of mind.

Cayce says, "For, ever in the flesh and in the spirit, **Mind** is the builder." (3333-1)

Being thankful takes your consciousness to a new level of awareness. It is an expression of the heart, and because it comes from the heart, people, yourself included, as well as the Light of the Creator, will respond positively.

Once we recognize that all of life's experiences have value, our thankfulness will automatically increase. Life's difficulties are man's doorways and pathways to further Light and endless joy. Without them, higher joys are not realized.

There is so much to be thankful for each and every day. There are many things we take for granted or perhaps don't even notice. The air that we breathe is one. The food we eat and water we drink are also important.

The blessing of food and drink aloud or silently before and after eating is important as well. It positively charges and changes their molecules.

The love we share with each other, something money can't buy, is most precious.

Sometimes we don't realize the gift of health until we are not well. When we recuperate, we thank God for our health. Why not thank Him now while we are feeling well?

I have found one of the greatest gifts in life to be thankful for is the ability to be of service. I ask God each day for His will to be made manifest through me and how I can serve Him.

There are times when people cross my path and I receive inspiration to help. Sometimes it would be just a kind word or a smile at a certain hour that would help lift someone's spirit (unbeknown to me that it was really what the person needed most just then). Other times, I might be prompted to pray for someone who comes to mind in need of prayer.

Edgar Cayce said, "Helping others is the best way to rid yourself of your own troubles." (5081-1)

We are all one, and what we do for others we do for ourselves. Great satisfaction can be felt in helping others on their life's journey.

4. Unconditional Love

Love encompasses patience, tolerance, thoughtfulness, meekness and kindness. It is of the Light, and can remove darkness of all kinds because of its enormous power. Love conquers all.

Before extending unconditional love to others, we need to give it to ourselves first. We cannot give away what we don't possess.

Forgiveness is the key to love. There is no other genuine way. In addition to forgiving is forgetting. This is true forgiveness with no shadows of resentment. *Remember Kabbalah teaches that this is only the one percent realm of our true reality.*

Our hearts are in need of love in all ways. We need to keep it open to receive the joy and fulfillment the Light of the Creator wants us to have. A closed heart blocks all of the Light and Love. Anger, bitterness, and animosity keep the heart closed.

Unconditional love, given to us by our Creator, keeps our heart open and frees us from much suffering and unnecessary pain. By being unconditionally loving and acting more like the

127

Creator, we are being proactive, an important key to bringing in more Light.

Because God is love, we are love, for we are part of Him. Love is our essence. There is a never ending supply. The more we give love, the more we receive. It works automatically.

Cayce put it this way. "<u>PRACTICE then in thy daily experience, and thy association with thy fellow man,</u> charity to all, love to all; finding fault with none; being patient with all, showing brotherly love and brotherly kindness. Against these there IS no law. And...by the application of them...ye become free of the laws that are of body or of mind; for ye are then conscious of being one <u>WITH</u> the Creative Forces that bring into the experience and consciousness of all the love of the Father for the children of men." (1620-1)

"What is it all about then? 'Thou shalt love the Lord thy God with all thine heart, thine soul, thine mind, thy body, and thy neighbor as thyself.' The rest of all the theories that may be concocted by man are nothing, if those are just lived." (3976-29)

The lyrics on the next page came to me when I needed to practice unconditional love. A wellspring of the Light's expansive love lifted me up as I heard these healing words of a spiritual nature.

"MY UNCONDITIONAL LOVE"

My Unconditional Love
Is a love that's found in the Spring
From the moment I saw you
My heart did adore you, and now it sings

My Unconditional Love
Is a love that's so very real
It's exciting, it's power
It's hour after hour, that's how I feel

No matter what you say or do
I'll still go on loving you
You're the moonbeam, the sunbeam
You're my dream
You light up my whole life

My Unconditional Love
Will grow more with each passing day
And if you'd look inside me
You'd see your love guide me in every way

Words and Music by Elliot Chiprut

5. Sharing

Kabbalah teaches that we are here only to make our corrections (Tikuns). By sharing the Light and creating unity and prosperity, we are acting more like the Creator. Sharing is a key ingredient to receiving properly. If we receive for the self alone, we are acting from our ego driven desire. When we receive in order to share, we become more God-like.

This is a very simple concept but a most important one. To receive in order to share brings more Light from the Creator and more to share. This works automatically. We shut down the flow when we receive only for the self. The opponent is the cause or root of the desire to receive for the self alone.

That is why the tithing principle is so important, giving at least a tenth of what we receive, be it in money, time, or material goods. It is an opportunity to share and be more in the flow of receiving as well. The Creator's supply of everything is boundless. We need to know and trust this truth.

At a higher level of awareness when we more fully understand that we are all One, we're actually giving more Light to ourselves when we share. There is no thought of separation or scarcity. Our remembrance that we are of the Light is actualized in materiality when we share. This is God in action.

Cayce broadens the concept with the following, "For all that ye may ever keep is just what you give away, and that you give away is advice, counsel, manner of life you live yourself... The manner in which you treat your fellow man, your patience, your brotherly love, your kindness, your gentleness that you give away, that is all that ye may possess in those other realms of consciousness." (5259-1)

In one Cayce reading, he advised: "Learn ye patience, if ye would have an understanding. If ye would gain harmony and grace in this experience!" (1201-2)

Kabbalah says through genuine actions of sharing and the giving of unconditional love, joy and fulfillment come. Not from what we expect in return.

The more we can properly share, the more we lessen our selfish nature and the darkness throughout the world. Being more God-like increases the Light everywhere.

The Light helps to refine and perfect our soul.

The Zohar states that perfection refers to the subjugation of the ego, and the transformation of the selfish desire to receive into a desire to receive for the sake of sharing.

Because sharing is the nature of the Light, when we share we take on the nature of the Creator. In effect, we become God-like, our true goal.

The Zohar also tells us that our primary purpose in life is to complete and perfect creation through our own spiritual transformation and growth. Sharing is an important key.

6. A Day of Rest

"And on the seventh day God ended His work which he had made; and He rested on the seventh day from all His work which He had made." Genesis 2:2

It is important to spend the seventh day of the week, normally Saturday or Sunday depending upon your belief, as a day of remembering the presence of the divine within you. This is done by taking a break from the material world. Connecting to this energy helps to purify our souls and enrich our lives.

The observing of the Sabbath, or Shabbat in Hebrew, according to the Jewish tradition, begins at sundown Friday night and ends Saturday after sundown.

This is a day of rest, no work and guilt free, which was commanded by the Creator and given to Moses in the Ten Commandments.

You are somewhat disconnecting temporarily from this third dimensional one percent world and connecting more with the 99% Upper World, bringing more of heaven to earth. Kabbalah states that Light usually has to be earned, but on the

Sabbath it is given as a free gift to all mankind who observe this holy day.

If you are interested in honoring this sacred time, a rewarding self-discipline, the simplest way to observe and celebrate the Sabbath is first to just be aware of it. For over nine years now, my wife and I have been observing the Sabbath each week, and have felt the peace and power of this twenty-four hour miracle. This is the time when the Sabbath angels from the Upper World are present in our midst. We invite them in when we begin the Sabbath.

In addition to feeling the *rest* of the Sabbath, we get to experience another gift, the blessings of the next six days as well. The Creator also designed the Sabbath to help us recharge our spiritual batteries. Kabbalah says the more we connect with the energy of the Sabbath, the smoother our lives will become. It is the one day during the week where the spiritual world and the physical world are united.

There is a powerful positive magnetic energy that is set up during the Sabbath that stays with you all week long. You can feel a difference. It may take a little getting used to at first to observe, because we're so accustomed to running around all week. On the Sabbath we find a true vacation from the everyday whirlwind and from our problems. It is proactive behavior as well, self-control, the discipline of following His commandment and bringing in more Light that we can now share with others.

You may want to first try observing it two or three times to experience the Sabbath's power and joy. Soon you will find that it can become a welcomed ritual. Participating and celebrating the Sabbath each week, allows us to connect with the energy of Light and to feel the gift of the Creator.

One of the main symbols of the Sabbath is white candles. Sabbath candles can be found inexpensively in most supermarkets. They are an emblem of the spiritual Light. If you are so inclined to include this tradition for the start of the Sabbath, light two candles Sabbath eve at sundown. This will enhance your Sabbath awareness. If a female is present, she should light the candles and pray the prayers, as others stand beside her.

One can simply say when lighting the candles, "These are the Sabbath candles."

Or, you may want to use the traditional Hebrew prayer: "Baruch atah Adonai eloheinu melech ha'olam asher kidshanu b'mitzvotav v'tzivanu lehadlik ner shel shabbat."

Or, the English translation: "Blessed are You, Lord our God, King of the universe, Who sanctified us with His commandments and commanded us to kindle the Sabbath candles."

The candles can also be placed on your dinner table or on a counter where they can be seen. They should be allowed to burn out on their own.

Other traditional elements you may want to add as you go along observing the Sabbath are the following: When lighting the candles, light them with a heartfelt intention. Remember, you are doing a commandment (mitzvah) and connecting with the Light of the Creator. After lighting the candles, if you are not alone, hug the person or persons next to you and greet them with "Shabbat Shalom," the Peace of the Sabbath.

During the Sabbath do what makes you feel refreshed, rested, and renewed. Take a nap. Go for a walk, especially in nature. Feed your soul with spiritual literature and poetry. Sing, play or listen to uplifting music. Dance. This is a time to celebrate. Eat plenty of delicious food. Relax. Working in the garden is a good activity. Nature heals. Try to stay close to home. Gather with friends and family if possible.

Do the things that are delightful. Forget the laundry for today. Try not to shop for anything. You will not find the Sabbath in the malls. If you must go to work on the Sabbath, try to observe the other parts of the Sabbath as much as you can. When the Sabbath is over, after it becomes dark, close the Sabbath by reading the 91st Psalm.

You can also add: "Blessed are you, Dear Lord, who separate the Holy from the secular." This prayer reconnects us back fully into the material world. Thank the Sabbath angels for being with you.

With a little practice, you'll be amazed at how wonderfully different you will begin to feel about yourself, others, and the world around you.

7. Humor and Laughter

An excellent fun and easy way to distance yourself from all types of problems is to inject humor and laughter. This helps to clear the air and release tension.

Laughter is a spiritual emotion that puts a healing smile upon your face. It gets rid of depression, worry, doubt, and aggravation. To laugh at your problems doesn't mean to ignore them, for that would be irresponsible. But while going through the process, the most effective way to find solutions to our problems is to not dwell on them.

Answers come when your mind is clear to receive. If you will learn to laugh more often and smile, you can clear your mind and enjoy life better by receiving more Light from the Creator.

Humor is the key that unlocks your laughter from within. When you can see humor in the unexpected, you can laugh.

When something absurdly funny happens and you are caught off guard, it can evoke laughter. Go with it. Something physiological also happens inside when you laugh that adds to your emotional health and well-being.

As mentioned before, the mind cannot serve two masters, so you can't be laughing and worried at the same time. It is impossible to entertain two separate thoughts simultaneously.

The idea for humor in balance is expressed in this Cayce reading. "The entity should attempt seriously, prayerfully, spiritually to see even that as might be called the ridiculous side of every question, the humor in same. Remember that a good laugh, an arousing even to what might in some be called hilariousness is good for the body physically, mentally and gives the opportunity for greater mental and spiritual awakening." (2647-1)

Another Cayce reading said, "It is by thy smile and not a word spoken, that the day may be brighter for many a soul and in making the day brighter, even for the moment, ye have contributed to the whole world of affairs." (2794-3)

Both humor and laughter are catalysts for building positive energy. When you tell a joke, hopefully in good taste, and bring a smile to others, you are also helping yourself. It is a part of our sharing Light and being proactive.

The Zohar says that laughter arouses immediate and direct pleasure. During spiritual tests, laughter ensures that hardships pass quickly and easily. It helps us regain control of our own happiness, rather than surrendering to external circumstances.

137

Cayce says, "See the humor in any experience, whether it is the most sacred, the most cherished experience, or that which comes as a trial." (2560-1) He also said, "Man alone in God's creation is given the ability to laugh." (2995-1)

One of the ways that can help you learn to laugh more is to remember what Kabbalah says about our reality on earth. *It is only one percent of our true reality.*

This can give the relativity needed to not get so caught up in anything. Remember, this too shall pass. Keep your vision on God. You will soon see that all will be made right. This is a truth that can be trusted.

The following is a little humor I found from Rabbi Weinberg, Rosh Yeshiva of Aish Hatorah, to help brighten the day:

A man is riding his motorcycle down a mountain road. Suddenly he loses control and goes hurtling off the cliff. As he's sailing through the air, he shouts out: "God! Please make a miracle! Save me!"

Moments later his shirt gets caught on a protruding branch, leaving him dangling thousands of feet above the ground. There's no way out, so he looks heavenward and shouts: "God! Please save me!"

"Do you trust Me, My beloved son?" calls the voice from heaven.

"Yes, God, I trust you. Just please save me."

"Okay then," says God. "Let go of the branch and I'll catch you."

The man thinks for a moment, looks around, and calls out: "Is anyone else out there?!"

8. Angel Power

From the Zohar, we learn there is a "vast system of angels which form a communication network through which positive and negative influences travel. This network acts as an interface between the physical world and the Upper Worlds."

"Everything in the physical world is governed by angels, including every blade of grass, every creature in the sea, and mankind as well. Because our powers of perception are severely limited, the power of the angels is as invisible as the force of gravity. The influence of both, however, is quite real."

"Everything positive that occurs in our lives is a direct result of positive angels."

"Likewise, all blockages, turmoil, difficulties and distress are the result of influences of negative angels."

"Our own behavior determines which angelic influences are aroused in the world."

Cayce had this to say about angels: "When thou hast shown in thine heart thy willingness to be guided and directed by **His** force, He gives His angels charge concerning thee. (423-3)

Car trouble can sometimes bring out the worst in us. If we can remember to apply the wisdom of Kabbalah and Cayce, we can have a smoother ride.

Several years ago during the hot summer months, I had to face an embarrassing situation. My 86-year-old mother-in-law was a backseat passenger as she traveled with us to our home in Virginia Beach for a weeklong visit. Halfway there our car made a strange noise and started losing power on the highway. Luckily we were right at the Toano Exit on I-64, and coasted down the ramp, calling out to the angels for help. We all laughed nervously as we successfully rolled into a McDonald's parking lot where the engine died. We were so grateful not to be stranded on the highway in the heat of the summer.

While waiting for Triple A, we decided to make the most of it and enjoyed lunch in the cool air conditioned golden arches. An hour later, the *Rocky Road Towing Company* showed up. There had been a lot of emergencies that morning. As it turned out, our car needed to be towed. There was only enough room in the truck cab for Karen and her Mom. I chose to ride in our car on top of the flat bed truck. Curious customers gathered around, watching us depart. Rather than get upset or embarrassed, we created a fun memory. I rolled down the window and waved to the crowd. Karen tried to take a picture of me on the flatbed for posterity, but the camera didn't work either.

The tow truck took us down the back roads of Williamsburg to the garage. The windows in the cab were rolled down and Karen noticed an angel ornament on the truck's rearview mirror twirling in the wind. She told her Mom the angels were still with us. At the garage, we learned a new transmission was needed. However, our day had an unexpected blessing. Karen's brother, David, who lived nearby, picked us up and took us back to his home. We enjoyed a wonderful evening with him and his family, going out to dinner and staying over for the night. It all worked out smoothly, as we rented a car and ours was towed back to the beach for repair.

The Edgar Cayce readings had much to say about help from the spiritual plane. In answer to this question: "Will I be able to have protection and guidance from the spirit plane to help me carry out my ideals for my best development in this life?" he said the following:

"If there is the finding of self in its relationships to the spiritual life, and the guiding of self therein; as given. Then do the angels and the guards in the spiritual life protect those in their activities." (405-1)

Cayce had good news for those searching for the light in the darkness. "The guardian angel--that is the companion of each soul as it enters into a material experience--is ever an influence for the keeping of that attunement between the creative energies or forces of the soul-entity **and** health, life, light and immortality…" (1646-1)

A good way to entertain the angels was brought out in this reading when Cayce explained, "Make thine home, thine abode, where an angel would DESIRE to visit, where an angel would seek to be a guest. For it will bring the greater blessings, the greater glories, the greater contentment, the greater satisfaction; the glorious one with another harmony of adjusting thyself and thy relationships one with another in making same ever harmonious. Do not begin with, 'We will do it tomorrow - we will begin next week – we will make for such next year.' Let that thou sowest in thy relationships day by day be the seeds of truth, of hope, that as they grow to fruition in thy relationships, as the days and the months and the years that are to come go by, they will grow into that garden of beauty that makes indeed for the home." (480-20)

It is comforting to know that there are angels all around us. Keeping a positive attitude both in word and deed will help insure their presence. I call upon my Guardian Angel and the Archangels Michael, Gabriel, Raphael and Uriel for their love and protection every day. They are Light bearers ready to serve us whenever we call upon them.

"ANGELS WATCHING OVER YOU"

There are angels in the park
There're angels everywhere you go
There're angels after dark it's true
Yes no matter where you are
The angels they're surrounding you
To whisper something light and new
Even if you're unaware
The angels how they care
To brighten up your point of view
There are Angels Watching Over You

There are angels in your house
They go along with you to work
There're angels in the classroom too
When you're shopping at the mall
The angels stand so very tall
They'll help you, call on them please do
Even if you're unaware
The angels how they care
To brighten up your point of view
There are Angels Watching Over You

Words and Music by Elliot Chiprut

Edgar Cayce's Angel Encounter

In the wonderful classic book, *There Is A River,* mentioned earlier, Thomas Sugrue tells of the time when Edgar Cayce was a young boy growing up in Kentucky. He had built a retreat in the woods behind his house. It was a lean-to made out of saplings, fir branches, moss, bark, and reeds from the edge of the brook. Cayce placed it by the willows where the stream took a bend. One afternoon in May as he was reading his Bible, sitting at the entrance of his lean-to, he noticed the presence of someone. When he looked up, he saw a woman standing in front of him, who at first he thought was his mother. The sun was bright and he didn't see well after staring at his book. However, when she spoke he didn't recognize the voice. It was soft and very clear, reminding him of music.

She said, "Your prayers have been heard. Tell me what you would like most of all, so that I may give it to you." Cayce saw there was something on her back that made shadows behind her, shaped like wings. He became frightened. She smiled at him and waited. He was fearful his voice would not make a sound, as it did in dreams.

When he opened his mouth, he heard himself saying: "Most of all I would like to be helpful to others, and especially to children when they are sick."

Cayce's wish has been granted over the years, and still is, with so many people, children included, being healed through the information in his readings.

Angel On The Bus

Many years ago, I was working in a photographer's studio. One day, while my car was in the repair shop, I needed to take the bus to work. The weather forecast for that day called for rain, so I took my umbrella. While waiting for the bus, I sat down on a nearby bench. At the far side of the bench sat an elderly man dressed in old, wrinkled, dirty clothes. He needed a shave and a bath. I sat on the bench and ignored him. Soon it started raining and I opened my umbrella. The elderly man on the other end was getting wet. I heard an inner voice say, "Go sit next to him and share your umbrella."

Reluctant at first, I then moved next to him to help keep him dry. To my surprise, we had a nice chat and he thanked me as the bus came. When we boarded the bus, he went toward the back and I sat near the front. There weren't many people on the bus. When I turned around to look at him, to my amazement, he was gone! There had been no stops along the way. I wondered then if he had been an angel? Cayce had this to say about angels, "Oft does man entertain angels unawares." (3011-3)

9. Water

According to Kabbalah, water is the Light of God made manifest in the physical world. Our bodies consist of over 65 percent water. The importance of pure water for both our physical and spiritual bodies cannot be underestimated. It will help to heal us and keep us young.

As one of the four earth elements, water can greatly benefit us not only physically but psychically as well. Water dissolves negativity. It helps to flush out our system and remove toxins, assuring the necessary elimination to achieve perfect health. Drink it pure and bathe or wash in it as often as you can.

The Cayce readings emphasized the importance of water. "...keep the body physically, mentally *clean,* in that those of pure water give life, vital forces, both internally and externally." (5613-1)

Drinking water is often just a matter of remembering to do so. By drinking water, we are also taking in the Light of our Creator.

The River Of Love

There is a river and it runs through each of us. I call this The River of Love. It is the Power of God. Strong and loving, its moving waters take us each and every day to the right places. Sometimes the river runs fast and we experience the rapids. This is when things in life are moving ever so quickly and we literally need to hold on. At other times, the river is calm and things slow down. We are still experiencing movement, but not too noticeably.

Knowing that The River of Love is constantly moving us back home to Oneness is comforting for me. I know it to be true. We don't always recognize that God's River of Love is constantly moving. No matter what is going on in our lives, we are part of this wonderful process of evolution. We can't help but get to our destination, sooner or later. The mighty River of Love never fails.

The Light of the Creator knows where we need to be at any given moment. The Light also knows and shows us how to get there when we ask. Yes, we indeed have choices and The River of Love gets us there even if some of our choices cause us to hit up against the rocks. Victory is assured. The River of Love flows and flows. It is unstoppable. All we need to do is allow the river to move us. There is nothing to fear. Try to feel The River of Love at this very moment. It is here. It beckons you to come home, as it welcomes you into the sea of eternity.

Chapter 9

SUMMING IT UP

To sum it up, the world we perceive with our five senses is not our true reality. It represents only one percent of our reality. Using the tools of Kabbalah, through meditation and prayer, and wisdom from the Edgar Cayce readings, we can become more attuned to the Real World where our Divine Self resides eternally.

It is through the opportunity of our everyday activities that we can witness what is the truth for us and grow inwardly. The Zohar teaches that in the manifestation of all things, some action is required on our part to arouse the activity from above. We must take inspired action. This will create our miracle.

When we overcome our ego's need to be selfish, leaving us in the dark and separate, we will attract more of the Light and remove the negative energy that keeps us in chains. If we proactively pursue to change our behavior and ask to become channels for the Light, by sharing, the effort will be well worth it. The result will be more peace and more happiness.

When we can rise above our problems first in our mind by asking the Light for help, our problems will then be removed.

The closer you walk with God, the closer God walks with you.

APPENDIX:

The Hebrew Alphabet Oracle

This oracle is based on the powerful energy of the Hebrew Alphabet and can also be used as a tool for transformation. Meditating on the Hebrew letters is a most inspiring way to connect to the divine world. The study of these letters was a method used by the early Kabbalists to penetrate the secrets of the cosmos.

The Zohar states that the twenty-two letters of the Hebrew alphabet were taken from the shape of constellations on the ecliptic and were thus letters of flame. Each letter of the Hebrew alphabet is a flame or combinations of flames and represents a certain type of cosmic energy used by the Creator to create the universe.

The core of this power can be found by observing the shape of each letter, connecting us to a higher realm of consciousness on the Tree of Life. The Hebrew letters are very much like DNA according to the Zohar, in that they are the spiritual genetic information through which all existence comes into being.

The oracle can be used for specific guidance to a question, or for everyday wisdom. Become quiet for several minutes. Take a few deep breaths.

Formulate a question in your mind. Avoid "yes" or "no" questions. Pray for inspiration and receptivity. Then simply open this section (pages 153 to 174) at random to choose a Hebrew letter and read the guidance given.

Meditate on the essence of the letter. Be sure to pay attention to any synchronicities that may appear regarding your selection. Let the Light of the Creator help you.

You may also want to make your own deck of Hebrew alphabet cards to access the oracle. (See instructions on page 175.)

1. ALEPH

FIRST LETTER OF THE ALPHABET:
Aleph represents the masculine aspect of the Creator and is seen as a link between the Creator and Its creation. Aleph symbolizes what is above can also be found below. Aleph also represents Unity. It stands for the Hidden Seed. Its power is generated through self-control.

NUMERICAL VALUE: One

SYMBOL: Ox or a Bull, the physical body, the physical plane.

KEYWORD: Perfection.

GUIDANCE: A breath of new life is stirring upon the waters of your soul. It is time for a new beginning. Plant your seeds. Be creative and original with your thoughts. Expect the best.

2. BET (or Beth)

SECOND LETTER OF THE ALPHABET:
The formation of the letter Bet is like an open, square house. Bet symbolizes a house, which contains the Spirit. It represents the feminine aspect of God.

NUMERICAL VALUE: Two.

SYMBOL: House.

KEYWORD: Formation.

GUIDANCE: Your body is a temple of God, for the presence of God dwells within it. Practice balancing body, mind and spirit. Cooperate with others to accomplish your goals. Give thanks even if you think you have little to be thankful for. Still your mind and remember God is the source of all things.

3. GIMEL

THIRD LETTER OF THE ALPHABET: Manifestation of Ideas. The focal point of the Trinity, composed of three numbers. The number 1 is masculine and number 2 is feminine. In order to create you need a positive and a negative to make a polarity. Gimel is a letter of abundance.

NUMERICAL VALUE: Three.

SYMBOL: Camel, Bridge, Good Deeds.

KEYWORD: New Life.

GUIDANCE: All things are born out of a trinity. Father, Mother, and Child. The Father is the Spirit and the mother is the physical. Creation can be seen in all life that surrounds you. Create your dreams through the seeds of Thought. Be conscious of all you think, for you are creating. When you are not in balance, you create negative situations. These signs ask you to get back into balance. If you have stepped out of connection with the Light of the Creator, ask yourself, "What am I creating? Why am I creating this?" Ask to be a channel for the Light.

155

ד

4. DALET

FOURTH LETTER OF THE ALPHABET:
The Dalet is constructed of two lines and a corner point. The word Dalet means door or poor. It characterizes the awareness of having nothing of one's own.

NUMERICAL VALUE: Four.

SYMBOL: Open Door. This is another symbol of the physical plane; you come through the door into the open. Man with his impulses and passions, must pass through door after door, in life after life, until he attains his ultimate goal, to be like the Divine.

KEYWORD: Aspiration.

GUIDANCE: You stand on the threshold of a new doorway. Release the past and bless it, for it led you to where you are today. Get your affairs in order and prepare to pass through the door into a new dimension of your life.

ה

5. HEI (or He, Hey, Heh)

FIFTH LETTER OF THE ALPHABET:
Hei is expression, thought, speech, and action. Giving to others is the utmost gift of Self. The importance of this letter is shown as it occurs twice in the sacred Tetragrammaton Yud Hei Vav Hei, the Name of God.

NUMERICAL VALUE: Five.

SYMBOL: Window. The Light coming through the window.

KEYWORD: Illumination.

GUIDANCE: If we should slip and fall, don't despair. The letter Hei also has a small opening near the top. This indicates not to give up. There is a way in which we can always climb back up out of the dark and return to the Light. Listen and trust.

ו

6. VAV

SIXTH LETTER OF THE ALPHABET:
The letter Vav is constructed of a vertical line. It joins things together. That is its secret. It has the appearance of an upright person, symbolic of humanity.

NUMERICAL VALUE: Six.

SYMBOL: Nail or Hook.

KEYWORD: Connection.

GUIDANCE: Think about what you would like to have happen in your life. Get in touch with your heart. Imagine how you would feel if you obtained your goal. Try to experience these feelings and hold on to them for they will attract your desire. If you are currently experiencing an aspect of life in which you are dissatisfied, try to connect with your thoughts about what is happening. You may notice that you have a lot of fear surrounding this issue. Ask to be a channel for the Light. Step out in faith. Do not be deceived by your five senses.

ז

7. ZAYIN

SEVENTH LETTER OF THE ALPHABET:
Zayin represents mysticism, spiritual integration, intuition, deep insight and the power of the Word.

NUMERICAL VALUE: Seven, the number of perfection.

SYMBOL: The Sword, Crown, Scepter.

KEYWORD: Victory.

GUIDANCE: With the sword of victory, cut away what no longer serves you. Whatever you need to release, give thanks for the opportunity it presented to help you transform your ego and receive more Light in your life.

8. CHET

EIGHTH LETTER OF THE ALPHABET:
The letter Chet shows two pillars crossed with a third, resembling a doorway with posts and lintel. Two other similar letters are Hei and Tav, but only Chet has the perfect balance of the two pillars upon which the crossbeam rests.

NUMERICAL VALUE: Eight.

SYMBOL: Fence or a Field of Cosmic Possibilities.

KEYWORD: Power.

GUIDANCE: Truly know that you can live the truth of your identity as a channel for the Light of the Creator. In exact proportion to what you send forth, so in good measure will it be returned to you. Practice being proactive by sharing. Look for ways to be a blessing to others.

9. TET

NINTH LETTER OF THE ALPHABET:
Tet represents potential power and looks like a serpent. The coiling of the serpent indicates a building up in man of spiritual energies that when released creates a heightened awakening to his divine origin.

NUMERICAL VALUE: Nine.

SYMBOL: Serpent.

KEYWORD: Ending (of a Cycle).

GUIDANCE: Make every effort to show up in order for your life to change.   Ask for the highest good to unfold.   Remember no one can take away what rightfully belongs to you. Change your approach.   Let go of fixed ways of being and acting. Make a commitment to face your fears and let go of cherished attitudes.   You are on the verge of a major transformation, bringing more Light to your soul.

י

10.   YUD (or Yod)

TENTH LETTER OF THE ALPHABET:
Every letter is made up of Yuds.   It is the smallest
letter in the alphabet and the only one suspended in
mid air. Yud is most important as it is the first letter
of the Holy Name of God, YUD HEI VAV HEI.

NUMERICAL VALUE: Ten.

SYMBOL: The Open Hand or God in Action.

KEYWORD: Divine Wisdom.

GUIDANCE: Study the letter Yud. Now close
your eyes and focus on Yud.   Listen to its divine
wisdom. Find the Light in your present circumstance.
See the Hand of the Creator using it for good.

11. CAF (or KAPH)

ELEVENTH LETTER OF THE ALPHABET:
The letters from Aleph to Yud represent the numbers 1 to 10. With Caf, the number does not coincide with the placement of that letter in the alphabet. Although Caf is the eleventh letter, it was written as the number 20. The first ten letters, like the Ten Commandments, show the path for the masses. Cosmic Law reflects in the Ten. With the eleventh letter the tests and trials begin the narrow way of Initiation.

NUMERICAL VALUE: 20.

SYMBOL: Palm of Hand, Grasping Hand. The hand is a channel for the flow of spiritual power, both incoming and outgoing.

KEYWORD: Strength.

GUIDANCE: Stretch out your hand to grasp the Light in the lesson. Give thanks that you are being healed. What was hidden is now being revealed. You are more than you know.

12. LAMED

TWELFTH LETTER OF THE ALPHABET:
Lamed is the tallest of all the Hebrew letters. Its
energy is able to bring down strong values to our
everyday existence. The word means to learn, to
teach. A heart that understands wisdom. It
symbolically means, "Thy Will, not my will, be
done."

NUMERICAL VALUE: 30.

SYMBOL: Ox Goad.

KEYWORD: Sacrifice.

GUIDANCE: Take responsibility for what you've
learned by sharing it with others. It is also an
important time to study, read and write. Be
encouraged to progress toward your goal in life. Use
more of your imagination to break through your
limitations of rational thinking.

13. MEM

THIRTEENTH LETTER OF THE ALPHABET:
The letter Mem denotes the Mother as the great Sea of Life out of which all life sprung forth. The fountain of Divine Wisdom.

NUMERICAL VALUE: 40.

SYMBOL: Water.

KEYWORD: Transformation.

GUIDANCE: The living waters of life support you. Spend time in or near water, giving thanks for its gift. Get into connection with the ocean, for your thoughts are like the waves that will eventually reach the shore. The shore is your physical life, the place of physical manifestation. Create the waves that you want to reach the shore. A purification is in process. Drink plenty of water.

14. NUN

FOURTEENTH LETTER OF THE ALPHABET:
The word Nun in Aramaic means fish. In Hebrew it means kingdom. It denotes humility. Nun is also the giver of wisdom.

NUMERICAL VALUE: 50.

SYMBOL: Fish.

KEYWORD: Initiate.

GUIDANCE: You are an Initiate. Be like the fish with your eyes ever open, swimming in a sea of abundance. Bring a blessing to others with your presence. Be of service to those in need.

15. SAMECH

FIFTEENTH LETTER OF THE ALPHABET:
The shape of the letter Samech is round and closed like a circle or wedding ring. Samech means support. The constant reassurance we are not alone.

NUMERICAL VALUE: 60.

SYMBOL: Prop or Support.

KEYWORD: Protection.

GUIDANCE: Gaze into the center of Samech and open yourself up to the portal of endless opportunities. Know that you can rely on the support of the Light of the Creator as you follow your inner promptings to fulfill your life's purpose. Call on the angelic realm for assistance. A miracle awaits you.

16. AYIN

SIXTEENTH LETTER OF THE ALPHABET:
The letter Ayin is formed from a Nun with an
extended foot and Vav (some say Zayin) resting in
the bend. The tops are compared to the right and left
eyes of a person. Through the eye we gain insight.

NUMERICAL VALUE: 70.

SYMBOL: Eye.

KEYWORD: Sudden Change.

GUIDANCE: Try to see a situation that has been
bothering you being resolved through the Eye of God.
When you see the Light of Truth, you understand that
you are solely responsible for the life you are living.
And only you have the power through your free will
to change this life.   Focus your energy on what you
want instead of what you do not want. Evaluate what
is not in your best interest, nor in alignment with your
soul.   You are a channel for the Light.

17. PEI (or Pey)

SEVENTEENTH LETTER OF THE ALPHABET:
Pei means mouth. It is formed from a Caf with a Yud attached to the upper lip, like a tongue. Through the mouth we bring to fruition that which is seen through the eye. The inner space of the letter Pei forms the letter Bet which symbolizes blessings.

NUMERICAL VALUE: 80.

SYMBOL: Mouth or Spoken Word.

KEYWORD: Communication.

GUIDANCE: Watch your words closely. The tongue wields much power. Remember, sometimes silence is golden. Use your voice as a healing balm to sooth an anxious world. As you speak loving words, you invite the Light of the Creator to enter and bless your relationships.

18. TZADI

EIGHTEENTH LETTER OF THE ALPHABET:
The shape of the Tzadi is formed from a bent Nun with a Yud on its back. The word Tzadi means to hunt. It also represents the Tzadikim, the righteous ones.

NUMERICAL VALUE: 90.

SYMBOL: Fishing Hook.

KEYWORD: Brotherhood/Sisterhood.

GUIDANCE: Trust in what is yet to be seen. Walk in faith that all is well with your soul. Help someone else on the path. Search for the truth and be open to all possibilities. You can access the power of the Light to actualize your potential.

19.   KOF (Or Kuf)

NINETEENTH LETTER OF THE ALPHABET:
The two letters Resh and Zayin together form the
letter Kof. The name stands for holiness. It is related
to the blending of the male and female polarities
within the body.

NUMERICAL VALUE: 100.

SYMBOL: Back of the Head.

KEYWORD: The Presence, God.

GUIDANCE: Expect a breakthrough in a
troublesome area of your life. The Light will come
streaming forth in unexpected creative ways bringing
great clarity. You will be able to discover holiness
within the ordinary. See the big picture.

20. RESH

TWENTIETH LETTER OF THE ALPHABET:
Resh is formed by the letter Vav leaning away from
the letter Kuf. Some people say it looks like a person
bent over. This letter represents the end of the
struggle for self-mastery.

NUMERICAL VALUE: 200.

SYMBOL: Head. The intellect, that which gives
conscious direction.

KEYWORD: Redemption.

GUIDANCE: Face the Light and let the shadows
fall behind you. The past is over and all that is left is
a blessing. Rely more on your inner promptings now.
Trust. A deeper, new beginning is at hand.

21. SHIN

TWENTY-FIRST LETTER OF THE ALPHABET:
The letter Shin is formed with three Vavs rising from a common base, each with a flaming Yud on top. It is often likened to a three pronged molar tooth, or the top half of a person reaching their arms up to heaven. Shin also illustrates the middle way between two opposites.

NUMERICAL VALUE: 300.

SYMBOL: Tooth.

KEYWORD: Peace.

GUIDANCE: Light a candle and meditate on the flame. Remember the Divine spark of the Creator resides in you. Make a commitment to work on removing any obstacles that could be holding you back from the Light.

22. TAV

TWENTY-SECOND LETTER OF THE ALPHABET:
Tav is comprised of a Dalet joined to a Nun. This
signifies the Initiate entering the doorway to the
physical world to do the soul's work of redemption.
Tav is also said to resemble a stamp or a seal. It is
the last letter of the Hebrew alphabet.

NUMERICAL VALUE: 400.

SYMBOL: T-shaped Cross.

KEYWORD: Completion.

GUIDANCE: The seal of completion is presented
to you. Release the outcome to the Light of the
Creator, knowing you did your best.

HOW TO CREATE YOUR OWN
HEBREW ALPHABET ORACLE DECK

To create your own oracle deck, photocopy the next page and cut out each letter with the number attached. The reference number will help you locate the letter in the oracle. Paste each individual letter with the number on a 3x5 card to create the deck.

Use the method on page 151, pick a card, and then refer to the oracle section for an answer.

ד 4	ג 3	ב 2	א 1
ח 8	ז 7	ו 6	ה 5
ל 12	כ 11	י 10	ט 9
ע 16	ס 15	נ 14	מ 13
ר 20	ק 19	צ 18	פ 17
		ת 22	ש 21

176

Bibliography

Ashcroft-Nowicki, Dolores. *Illuminations: Mystical Meditations On The Hebrew Alphabet.* St. Paul, Minnesota: Llewellyn Publications, 2003.

bar Yochai, Rabbi Shimon. *The Zohar.* New York, NY: Kabbalah Centre International Inc., 2003.

Berg, Kabbalist Rav. *Kabbalistic Astrology.* New York, NY: Kabbalah Centre International Inc., 2000.

Berg, Michael. *Becoming Like God.* New York, NY: Kabbalah Centre International Inc., 2004.

Berg, Yehuda. *Power of Kabbalah.* New York, NY: Kabbalah Centre International Inc., 2000.

Berg, Yehuda. *The 72 Names of God: Technology For The Soul* ™. New York, NY: Kabbalah Centre International Inc., 2004.

Berg, Yehuda. *The Kabbalah Book Of Sex: & Other Mysteries Of The Universe.* New York, NY: Kabbalah Centre International Inc., 2006.

Braun, T.T. *The Power In Thank You.* Cedar City, Utah: Wisdom Digest Publishing, 2004.

Cerminara, Gina. *Many Mansions.* New York, NY: William Sloane Associates, Inc., 1950.

Corinne, Heline. *The Bible and the Tarot.* Marina del Rey, CA: DeVorss & Co., 1989.

Chu, Chin-ning. *Do Less, Achieve More.* New York, NY: Harper Collins Publishers, Inc., 1998.

Farley, Nelson L. *A Search For God Paraphrased.* Painter, VA: The Ink Drop Press, 1998.

Frejer, Ernest B. *The Edgar Cayce Companion.* Virginia Beach, VA: A.R.E. Press, 1995.

Kaplan, Aryeh. *Sefer Yetzirah: The Book Of Creation.* York Beach, ME: Samuel Weiser, Inc., 1997.

Ponce', Charles. *Kabbalah, An Introduction and Illumination for the World Today.* Wheaton, IL: The Theosophical Publishing House, 1978.

Puryear, Herbert B. *The Edgar Cayce Primer.* New York, NY: Bantan Books, Inc., 1982.

Sasson, Gahl and Weinstein, Steve. *A Wish Can Change Your Life.* New York, NY: a Fireside Book (Simon & Schuster), 2003.

Sechrist, Elsie. *Meditation: Gateway To Light.* Virginia Beach, VA: A.R.E. Press, 2004.

Sugrue, Thomas. *There Is A River: The Story of Edgar Cayce.* Virginia Beach, VA: A.R.E. Press, 1942.

Think on These Things: Timeless Wisdom from the Edgar Cayce Readings. Virginia Beach, VA: A.R.E. Press, 1981.

White Eagle. *The Quiet Mind.* Hampshire, England: The White Eagle Publishing Trust, 1993.

Winston, Shirley Rabb. *Music As The Bridge.* Virginia Beach, VA: Edgar Cayce Foundation, 1972.

Additional Resources

Music From My Heart CD – Elliot Chiprut
Piano Solo - 13 original semi-classical/pop
inspirational compositions.

Amazing Grace CD – Elliot Chiprut
Piano Solo - 13 original inspirational compositions,
includes 7 inspirational waltzes, and the classic,
Amazing Grace.

Both CDs and this book are currently available at:
elliotchiprut.com.

Western Yoga For All – Guidelines From The Edgar Cayce Readings DVD – Peter Van Daam's Exercises. Simple postures, low impact, no mat (especially good for seniors), and takes 15 minutes. Benefits include: high energy, better overall health, improved balance, memory, alertness, and greater soul expression.

DVD available at: petervandaam.com
Email contact: peter.vandaam@yahoo.com

ABOUT THE AUTHOR

Elliot Chiprut was born into a Jewish family and raised in Brooklyn, New York. At the very early age of six-years-old, he learned to play the piano by ear. By the time he was twenty-four, he had earned two gold records, "Simon Says," which he wrote and co-produced, and "Little Bit O' Soul," which he co-produced. He has written over one thousand songs in many different genres.

Dissatisfied with the results of achieving fortune and fame in the material world to bring him happiness and peace, he reached out to learn about the spirit side of his true self. His soul searching led him to studying for many years, the Old and New Testament, Edgar Cayce, *A Course in Miracles*, Ascended Master Teaching, and Kabbalah. Along with meditation, this brought him the peace and happiness he desired and now shares.

Elliot happily lives the precepts of spirituality with his wife Karen and their cat Angel in Florida.

CPSIA information can be obtained at www.ICGtesting.com
Printed in the USA
BVOW002147270313

316671BV00006B/29/P